"The Truth shall Set you Free." (John 8:32)

# 77 Soundbytes of Love

The Philosophical Spirituality of Ronda Chervin

En Route Books and Media, LLC

Saint Louis, MO

En Route Books and Media, LLC
5705 Rhodes Avenue
St. Louis, MO 63109

Contact us at
**contact@enroutebooksandmedia.com**

Cover Credit: Sebastian Mahfood

Copyright © 2023 by Ronda Chervin

ISBN: 979-8-88870-052-5

Library of Congress Control Number: 2023940346

All rights reserved.

Printed in the United States of America. No part of this book may be used or reproduced in any manner whatsoever without written permission except in the case of brief quotations embodied in critical articles or reviews.

# What's Inside

Intro ........................................................................................................................ 1

DAY 1: Loving and Unloving Thoughts, Words and Deeds ........................... 4
DAY 2: Be gentle, patient, and peaceful! ........................................................ 6
DAY 3: Nothing is Perfect on Earth ................................................................ 8
DAY 4: Praying to the God of Love ............................................................... 10
DAY 5: Preparing for Confession ................................................................... 12
DAY 6: Walk don't Talk .................................................................................. 14
DAY 7: Rosary Mysteries in our Lives ........................................................... 16
DAY 8: Don't say I can't, say I won't! ............................................................ 18
DAY 9: A Meaningful Life .............................................................................. 20
DAY 10: Humor is your Best Friend .............................................................. 22
DAY 11: Speak the Truth with Love (Ephesians 4:15) - when talking about Controversial Issues ....................................................................... 24
DAY 12: What is your Bitter Root Judgment? .............................................. 26
DAY 13: Soaring or Rescue? ........................................................................... 28
DAY 14: Love is not loved .............................................................................. 30
DAY 15: Accepting Difference ....................................................................... 32
DAY 16: Forgiveness ....................................................................................... 34
DAY 17: Spiritual Friendship: the Darkness and the Light ......................... 36
DAY 18: Popularity ......................................................................................... 38
DAY 19: Frustrations with Tech .................................................................... 40

DAY 20: Why don't you Want to be my Friend? .......................................................... 42

DAY 21: "Our Hearts are Restless, until they find their Rest in Thee" (St. Augustine) ............................................................................................................. 44

DAY 22: How to Write your Memoirs for Family and Friends ............................... 46

DAY 23: "Humility is not thinking less of yourself but thinking of yourself less." C.S. Lewis ................................................................................................ 48

DAY 24: A Day of Giving Thanks .............................................................................. 50

DAY 25: Learning from Pets? ..................................................................................... 52

DAY 26: Joy at Holy Mass .......................................................................................... 54

DAY 27: Live in the Now ............................................................................................ 56

DAY 28: There is an Abyss between an Ardent Catholic and a Saint ................... 58

DAY 29: Dislike of Change ......................................................................................... 60

DAY 30: Why go to Confession? ................................................................................ 62

DAY 31: How Photo Collections on the Lap-top Screen Bring Joy ...................... 64

DAY 32: Looking Forward to Your Resurrected Body ........................................... 66

DAY 33: How our Relationship to our Parents and Family can affect our Relationship to God, the Father and Mary our Mother. ...................... 68

DAY 34: Padre Pio's Healing Prayer .......................................................................... 70

DAY 35: Excuses for Abortion ................................................................................... 72

DAY 36: The Child is the Love of the Parents made Visible .................................. 74

DAY 37: Passive Purification ...................................................................................... 76

DAY 38: Everlasting or Eternal? ................................................................................ 78

DAY 39: Becoming a Dedicated Widow ................................................................... 80

DAY 40: "You can only love yourself, loving." ......................................................... 82

DAY 41: Can we be Joyful even in the Midst of Tragedy? ...................................... 84

Introduction .................................................................................................................. 3

DAY 42: Will what you are about to say help me to love this person? ..................... 86

DAY 43: Personality Types – Helpful or Harmful? .................................................. 88

DAY 44: Called by Name: Following a Personal Spirituality ................................... 90

DAY 45: "Now and at the hour of our death" ........................................................... 92

DAY 46: Recovery International for Anger, Anxiety, and Depression ..................... 94

DAY 47: Games: Silly or Good? ................................................................................ 96

DAY 48: The Perfect is the Enemy of the Good ....................................................... 98

DAY 49: Pacifism A and B ....................................................................................... 100

DAY 50: What is the Theme? .................................................................................. 102

DAY 51: What is each of our Worst Defect? ........................................................... 104

DAY 52: Why do you Think Irrational People will be Rational? ............................ 106

DAY 53: Loving even when you can't Like??? ........................................................ 108

DAY 54: God alone is Enough ................................................................................. 110

DAY 55: Praying on Tippy-Toes or in the Heart ..................................................... 114

DAY 56: The Divine Within? ................................................................................... 116

DAY 57: Contraception - Why it is Wrong ............................................................. 118

DAY 58: Absolutizing Trivia ................................................................................... 120

DAY 59: Who Won the Battle for the 20th Century Mind? .................................... 122

DAY 60: Hobbies and Identity ................................................................................ 124

DAY 61: Jewish Converts ........................................................................................ 126

DAY 62: Jesus and I are 'Bigger' than myself and any only Human Person. .......... 128

DAY 63: "Stop Dogpaddling in the Waves of Life, let Me Float you to the Shore of Eternity" ............................................................................................................ 130

DAY 64: Doubts about the Catholic Faith? ............................................................. 132

## Twelve of my Favorites of my Books: Let me Tell you Why!

**DAY 65:** *The Church of Love* .................................................................................. 136

**DAY 66:** *Voyage to Insight* .................................................................................... 138

**DAY 67:** *Feminine, Free and Faithful* .................................................................... 140

**DAY 68:** *Kiss from the Cross: A Saint for Every Type of Suffering* .......................... 142

**DAY 69:** *En Route to Eternity: The Story of Ronda Chervin* ................................... 143

**DAY 70:** *Spiritual Friendship: The Darkness and the Light* ..................................... 144

**DAY 71:** *The Widow's Walk: How the Widow Saints bring comfort and direction* .. 145

**DAY 72:** *Taming the Lion Within: 5 Steps from Anger to Peace* ............................. 146

**DAY 73:** *The Way of Love* ..................................................................................... 147

**DAY 74:** *Last Call: Twelve Men who Dared Answer* ............................................... 148

**DAY 75:** *Why be an Atbeist if?* (co-author Sebastian Mahfood) ............................. 149

**DAY 76:** *Escaping Anxiety on the Road to Spiritual Joy* (co-author Al Hughes) ..... 150

**DAY 77:** *Always a New Beginning* (co-author David Dowd) ................................... 151

Good-bye .................................................................................................................. 153

Books I Wrote ........................................................................................................... 155

# Intro

Many years ago, my son, Charlie, rode out into the desert to see if Jesus would tell him a truth that would set him free.

After a day or two without a clear answer, he heard Jesus seem to say:

"Your mother writes a lot of books about these subjects.
Why don't you read one?"

After reading one, he came to me and exclaimed: "Gee, Mom, if you did what you tell people to do in your books, you would be a saint!"

Now, more than 30 years later, retired and looking for insights into how to become more holy, Jesus seemed to say to me:

"Ronda, you have the insights you need. Now live them!"

It came to me in the night of February 28, 2023, that it could be good to re-read my books and put together an anthology of soundbytes for me, and also for my readers. Each day we would try to live the truth in each soundbyte and briefly record our experience.

But! I then suddenly thought:

"Mama mia, how have I become so arrogant that, instead of leaving the collecting of excerpts to some disciple, I am thinking I, myself, should put together such a book?"

Hmmm! It is probably partly true that it would be more usual for a disciple to put together such a book.

However, I believe my best insights come from the Holy Spirit. Why? Because they are better than my own. And, throughout many decades, my readers have been helped by such truths.

So, I will make a try. Here is the format: Each day for 77 days there will be a soundbyte with a brief explanation. Then I will try to live by that truth all day long. I will journal insights from my day of living out the truth or ignoring it with poor results.

Then there will be space for you, the reader, to add insights. Feel free to include extra sheets of paper where the space is too small! Here is an example:

Day One: "Take note of loving and unloving thoughts, words and deeds that you see around you, including your own." (from *The Way of Love*)

**Ronda:**

        Loving                Unloving

**Insights:**

[My personal insights.]

**Reader:**

        Loving                Unloving

**Insights:**

[Your personal insights.]

# Introduction

**My prayer:**

Holy Spirit, I thank you for the inspiration to write many Catholic books that helped me and that readers tell me helped them. May this compilation of soundbytes push me and the reader further along on the road to union with the Holy Trinity and all the saints in heaven.

Note: Even though Soundbytes is divided into 77 days, it is not a lockstep! You can decide to skip some that don't apply. You can decide to spend 5 days on some soundbyte that is especially important to you requiring more than a day to exhaust its meaning.

Another Note: These soundbytes are no substitute for the essence of Catholic spirituality: the Holy Mass, the sacraments and scripture, the rosary. They always come first. The soundbytes are only contemporary ways of trying to allow the grace of God to more greatly impact our daily lives.

Already before the publication of *Soundbytes*, some interested Catholics wanted to read and share about them in a group. Dr. Sebastian Mahfood, OP, the publisher of En Route Books and Media thought it could be good to have a blog based on them on the web where readers could share as they read with me, the author, and others responding.

If you like this idea, check out enroutebooksandmedia.com/soundbytes.

Feel free to also email me at chervinronda@gmail.com.

## DAY 1: Loving and Unloving Thoughts, Words, and Deeds

"Take note of loving and unloving thoughts, words and deeds that you see around you, including your own." (from *The Way of Love*)

Ronda:

| Loving | Unloving |
|---|---|
| Thanking someone | Raising my voice |
| Offer of help | Critical thoughts |
| Looking up something for someone | Snappishness |
| Praying for someone aloud | Impatient ideas |
| Someone makes good dinner for others | |

Insights:

I realize that even if I am observing loving and unloving thoughts, words and deeds, unless I make being loving the highest priority in thought, word, and deed, I will react negatively often.

# Day 1: Loving and Unlovings Thoughts, Words, and Deeds

Reader:

        Loving                   Unloving

Insights:

## DAY 2: Be gentle, patient, and peaceful!

"This morning in prayer I felt more surrendered to You, dear Jesus, and eager to beg You to give me the gentleness and patience and peace that so elude me. You seemed to tell me that I cannot have peace until I accept the tiny crosses of everything each day that is antipathetical to me in any way.

So, dear Jesus, here is my prayer: I accept all those little annoyances as well as the big one of having to wait still much longer to try a particular new living situation. Please, dear Guardian Angel, remind me before each segment of my daily life that becoming surrendered and therefore peaceful in this way is more important than any projects. That it is my project!

(From *Latest Journal 2022*)

Ronda:

Insights:

I felt peaceful even early this morning planning on trying! I wanted to remind someone to do something but decided on patience and within the next hour it was done without my intervention. Instead of moving around quickly and jerkily, going more slowly through my day helps with peacefulness. I realize that rehearsing sarcastic thoughts about someone else's ways is not gentle!!!!

## Day 2: Be Gentle, Patient, and Peaceful!

Reader:

Insights:

## DAY 3: Nothing is Perfect on Earth.

"Everything has its advantages and disadvantages."

"Don't ask if some job or dwelling is perfect, ask if you can stand it!"
(from journals or *9 Toes in Eternity*)

These statements from mentors of mine are of great importance to me. They keep me from gyrating between fantasies of perfect alternatives to my various life situations. I believe that since becoming a widow some 30 years ago, I am called to be a kind of pilgrim. Just the same, there are times when it is better to stay where I am planted. In the 30 years since my husband's passing into eternity, I have lived in some 20 different places!

I will avoid writing about the pros and cons of living with family and specific friends. They probably wouldn't like to be described in this book. Instead, I am going to concoct a semi-fictional option to illustrate the maxims about everything having advantages and disadvantages and nothing being perfect. And you, dear reader, may try prayerfully to analyze some option that you are considering.

Ronda:

Insights:

One option is living close to family. The advantages or pros have to do with the pleasures of being with those I have known and loved for many decades and who, also, know me and love me. And that, in spite of my flaws and bad faults. So, what's the disadvantage? Each family has some different values which make it hard for them to be with me or for me to be with them.

The other option involves trying a lay community. Advantages are daily Mass in the Church next door to the residence and fellowship with those of the same Catholic values. Disadvantages are being far from family and the unpredictable possibly clashing defects of members with my defects.

Viewing these pros and cons I have to take in that nothing on earth is perfect. So, discernment has to weigh whether there is anything in either of those options I absolutely can't stand or not. As well, there is the hugeness of one or another of the positives that could make any disadvantages worth it.

Also, remembering past living situations I have to realize that I can't figure all this out as if it were a math problem.

"Wait and see," is what all my mentors advise me.


Reader:


Insights:

## DAY 4: Praying to the God of Love

"Truth is not an idea or a theory but a Person whose name was Love…for some prayer is like a duty, to be accomplished with mechanical regularity, as if it were, a tax paid to the creator for the good things in life…Some have not found Christ…they explore the unconscious self to find a faceless Deity within…yet in the depths of the heart everyone seeks a perfect lover to whom all secret thoughts and feelings can be revealed…we long for perfect love open-armed in forgiveness." (From *The Way, the Truth and the Life: Meeting Christ in Prayer*)

Any of us can slip into praying in the mechanical way I described above. Let us spend time today very consciously addressing our prayers of all kinds to the God of Love we know in Jesus.

Ronda:

Insights:

I see I need to pray set words such as in the Liturgy of the Hours, slowly not with any kind of quick deadline of a finishing line. Then there is room for the God of Love to make the words apply to my present state of mind.

I changed the masculine for David in the Psalms to the feminine for me "God will save her from her enemies."

# Day 4: Praying to the God of Love

Since my twin-sister, Carla De Sola, is a sacred dancer, she has taught me the goodness of even raising my arms openly to such verses as "into Your hands I commend my spirit."

Reader:

Insights:

## DAY 5: Preparing for Confession

On Examination of One's Faults and Sins:

Most readers of Soundbytes have been going to the sacrament of Confession for many years. Just the same, we may need fresh insights to deepen our participation such as those of St. Francis de Sales, a doctor of the Church.

"Be careful in confession to mention those details which explain the nature of your fault, such as the cause which excited your anger, or led you to encourage what was wrong. Thus, someone whom I dislike has said some trifles in jest, which I took amiss and was angry with him' but if a person I liked had said something more offensive, I should not have taken it amiss."

"Some make a great mistake who are angry because they have been angry, hurt because they have been hurt, and vexed because they have been vexed. Thus, whilst they fancy that they are ridding their breast of anger, and that their second passion remedies the first. In truth they are preparing the way for fresh anger on the first occasion; besides which, all this indignation and vexation and irritation with ourselves tends to foster pride, and springs entirely from self-love, which is displeased at finding that we are not perfect. We should endeavor then to look upon our faults with a calm, collected, firm displeasure."

From *A Diary of Meditations (from St. Francis de Sales)* edited by Dom Cuthbert Smith, O.S.B. (Chicago: Henry Regnery Co.:1957) pp. 23-24.

# Day 5: Preparing for Confession

Ronda:

Insights:

Regarding the quotation from St. Francis de Sales about being angry that I was angry, I am remembering a teaching of my godfather. He said, when we are outraged that we have sinned it is as if we thought we were almost saints already. More humble would be to say to oneself: "Here, I am, a sinner. I am sorry to have sinned again. Help me, Jesus."

Reader:

Insights:

## DAY 6: Walk don't Talk

A friend who read my little booklet *Talkaholics: Fate or Work in Process* told me that since he is bi-polar, talking is kind of manic. If he talks less, he gets depressed. Since I found that I felt more depressed as I practiced talking less, I asked how he prays through depression. To my surprise, he said that walking a lot was a great remedy.

Ronda:

Insights:

This plan corresponds to a tool used in Recovery, International (not 12 Step, founded by Abraham Low for anger, anxiety, and depression in the 1940's). When upset in different ways it is always good to:

Move your Muscles.

Why? Since we are mind/body composites as Aristotle put it long ago, our mental states can be easily influenced by our bodily states. So just as eating a delicious meal makes us feel happier, so walking or running or exercising can make us feel better in our minds and hearts.

Since I am very sedentary, I find it is always good to move around more. When the weather is cold I force myself to use my pedal pusher and I do feel better immediately.

Day 6: Walk, don't Talk

Reader:

Insights:

## DAY 7: Rosary Mysteries in our Lives

"As we dwell on the joyful, sorrowful, and glorious mysteries of Mary's tale, we will be exploring the way our own lives embody the same themes: joyful surprise, confirmation, celebration, homecoming, crying out, violence, resignation, pain, the wound of death, reunion, ecstasy, fire, the leap to heaven, and the fulness of the end times."
(*Bringing the Mother with You, Sources of Healing in Marian Meditation* with co-author Sister Mary Neill, O.P. (N.Y. The Seabury Press: 1982) p.7-8)

Ronda:

Insights:

When writing this book about the Rosary, so many years ago, I liked to ask myself on the days of each of the mysteries:

"Today, Ronda, what was the joyful mystery you experienced?" Perhaps the smile of my little child.

"Today, Ronda, what was the sorrowful mystery you experienced?" Perhaps a conflict over moral teachings with a student in my ethics class.

"Today, Ronda, what was the glorious mystery you experienced?" Perhaps being at Holy Mass.

Now I could ask about the luminous mystery. Perhaps a sun shining on the ocean.

## Day 7: Rosary Mysteries in our Lives

Reader:

Insights:

## DAY 8: Don't say I can't, say I won't!

A priest made this demand after listening to a long list from me of things I thought I couldn't bear in life. The point was that many times we think we can't do something good but hard and we really just won't because we don't want to.

I found in old age an application of this maxim in situations where I think I am too weak to do something and I really can such as opening a tight jar of juice. It might take a few minutes longer than when my hands were stronger, but it is still possible.

Ronda:

Insight:

A way I try to push myself to try harder when I think I can't do something is to ask:

If someone offered me $500 to do it, wouldn't I figure it out?

It always comes out that even though I think I can't I really can.

Example: I have a bad habit of picking my fingernails. It's so engrained that I hardly notice I am doing it. But, if you offered me $500 to bury one hand in my coat pocket at Holy Mass and not use it to pick the nails of the other hand, don't you think I would take the $500 and do it?

(See *9 Toes in Eternity*)

Day 8: Don't say I can't, say I won't!

Reader:

Insight: Try the $500 funny joke when you don't think you can do something of any kind and write about how it worked here.

## DAY 9: A Meaningful Life

"Everyone wants to have a meaningful life in which his or her unique talents contribute to the building of the kingdom of love."
(from *The Way, the Truth and Life: Meeting Christ in Prayer*)

I believe it is God who has given me gifts of teaching, speaking, and writing. Of course, sometimes I have made mistakes in these spheres but a lot of the time they have helped building our Catholic kingdom of love.

Ronda:

Insights:

    Even though my gifts are public and acknowledged, that doesn't mean they are the most important ways of building the kingdom of love. Sometimes a woman would come up to me after a lecture and begin her remarks by saying "I am only a housewife, but…" I would always stop her and ask her how many children she had. If she answered with a number higher than 3, I would insist:
    "I had 3 live children and 4 miscarriages. Which of your children who will live for all eternity would you exchange for a book written by you that will one day be thrown in a trash bin!"

# Day 9: A Meaningful Life

Reader:

Insight: Write here about gifts from God you have been given that contribute to the kingdom of love.

## DAY 10: Humor is your Best Friend

A tool in Recovery, International (not 12 Step) for anger, fear and depression is to tell oneself: "anger is my worst enemy, humor is my best friend." We are to look for a funny side to upsetting situations. (from *The Comic Catholic*)

Here are two of my favorite examples of absolutely unexpected humor. My teen daughter was in a class where the assignment was to devise a business card for someone. She picked me. At the time I was an Assistant Professor of Philosophy. Here is what she had on the card she designed for me:

Ronda Chervin, Ph.D., full time martyr, part time saint.

In another case, an English professor known for humorous pranks died after a long hospital stay. At the funeral his wife told us about his final prank. Just at the moment that the hospital called to report that Frank had died, at their house the toilet seat broke in two!

A friend of mine is writing her memoirs with the title "I Had to Laugh!"

Ronda:

Insights:

What helps me when I don't like long conversations between others about subjects I am not interested in, I ask myself, with a laugh: would I rather have puppets instead of friends so they would only talk with words I made them say?

# Day 10: Humor is Your Best Friend

Reader:

Insight: Write about some funny things that you have heard or said.

## DAY 11: Speak the Truth with Love (Ephesians 4:15) when talking about Controversial Issues

"No matter how vehemently you are convinced of the truth about matters such as certain moral teachings of the Church, when talking to those who disagree, speak the truth with love."
(from *The Crisis in the Church,* a semi-fictional dialogue.)

The opposite of speaking the truth with love is speaking the truth with hate. That may sound like too strong a word. But, consider, what is ridicule but a form of disgusted disdain?

The philosopher, Dietrich Von Hildebrand, wrote that the temptation for those of us who hold firmly to the truth is that we will enjoy "hurling denunciations from the throne of truth."

We take pride in being able to refute those on the other side, but, then, often by not lovingly listening to the other person, we risk putting them on the defensive. Then, they are less likely to take in the truth we want them to learn!

Ronda:

Insights:

Generally, I only fraternize with people who agree with me about most issues in the Church or in politics. When I have to be in the company of those who

# Day 11: Speak the Truth with Love (Ephesians 4:15)

disagree, I find it better not to yell out: "Here's why you're wrong!" Instead, when I say softly: "Here is how I came to see the truth," at least I don't totally alienate the other person!

Reader:

Insights:

## DAY 12: What is your Bitter Root Judgment?

One of my best books was written with Al Hughes, a Lieutenant Colonel in the Airforce who became a pastoral counselor and spiritual director after his retirement. It is called *Escaping Anxiety: Along the Road to Spiritual Joy*.

A central insight of Hughes about pervasive chronic anxiety is that it comes out of what he calls a bitter root judgment from childhood.

Example: when a child Al's father though a good, dutiful man, was what would later be diagnosed as clinically depressed. He came home from managing a sugar planation in Louisiana and hid behind the newspaper, shunting Al, his son, off to his own room to do his homework. Al's bitter root judgment was that he must be ugly and that was why his father didn't want to see him around!

Children bullied in school often think that they are stupid. Children of divorced parents often make the bitter judgment that the parent left not because of conflict with the spouse but because of them.

The remedy is to discover the bitter root judgment behind one's irrational anxieties. Then we are to bring this to Jesus for healing.

Ronda:

Insights:

When I am not simply concerned about a real problem, but irrationally anxious, it helps me to see if my bitter root judgment has been triggered. If the boss doesn't smile at me in the hall today, it doesn't mean I am about to be

# Day 12: What is your Bitter Root Judgment

fired! When the anxiety persists, it helps to bring it to prayer to Jesus who will never reject me unless I reject Him.

Reader:

Insights: (Note: If you find some resonance in these thoughts about the origin of irrational anxiety, I suggest you get hold of *Escaping Anxiety: Along the Road to Spiritual Joy* and ponder the teachings.)

## DAY 13: Soaring or Rescue?

A great Benedictine spiritual master made use of this image:

We want to think of our spiritual journey as if we were soaring from the bottom of a mountain up to the top. But, in reality, it is more like we start climbing the mountain and fall into a bramble bush. Jesus comes and rescues us and we start onward again. It is like a slow spiral up the mountain.

Ronda:

Insights:

When I first became a Catholic at 21, I imagined I would soar up the mountain of holiness right away! I was shocked that I had to confess some venial sins such as yelling at people, over and over again! That was my "bramble bush."

I always feel better after Confession, but still always fondly imagine that this will be the last time I confess to some recurring fault. It is as if I would finally soar right up to heaven.

Yet it would not be good to assume that I will sin again, as if it were fate! Just the same, how wonderful that Jesus comes down the mountain, as it were, and lifts me out of the brambles and smilingly sets me back on the path!

# Day 13: Soaring or Rescue?

Reader:

Insights: What is your bramble bush? Maybe write a little prayer thanking God for releasing you and setting you back on the path.

## DAY 14: Love is not loved.

"Love is not loved." This was a thought originally of St. Bernard of Clairvaux. I got those words myself once during prayer with this personal response of mine: "Love is not loved. Is it easier for me to love you as truth because truth is strong and love is vulnerable? Is it easier for me to love you as beauty because beauty is sublime and love is messy?"

Do I think that if I surrender to Love He will give me unbearable crosses to bear?" Jesus seemed to respond that "Mother Mary didn't emerge from surrender to you as a dead fish, but rather as Queen of Apostles!"

Or, I ask myself now, do I prefer admiration to love because I think I can earn it and love is gratuitous... (from *Journals 2001* – in *En Route to Eternity: Further along the Road*)

Ronda:

Insights:

What does this "Love is not loved" mean to me at this time of my life? I have had many admirers as a teacher, writer, and speaker. However, some of those closest to me in the present love me but do not particularly admire what I do in those roles. That makes me feel vulnerable. As I come into contact with such persons I need to ask Jesus to show me that this little cross of not being admired for the accomplishments, opens me to receive love for my person-

# Day 14: Love is not Loved. 31

hood in itself – flaws and all. A counselor of mine put it this way: Ronda, if when you are with others you stopped strutting your stuff, others would see your vulnerability and help you!"

Help me to be less concerned with how others react to me and, instead be more motherly to all like Mary is.

Reader:

Insight:

# DAY 15: Accepting Difference

I find that, on a daily basis, I feel upset about some trivial difference between my tastes, views, etc. and someone else's even if we are friends.

Examples: one woman prefers wearing pants, and I prefer wearing jumpers. One person believes in walking every day, and I am more sedentary. One person scrupulously recycles and I sometimes drop an item in the wrong bin.

Now I am not writing about huge evils and sins. Accepting differences doesn't mean shrugging one's shoulders when hearing about Hitler's holocaust!

But how unloving is it to argue with others about trivial differences, or concoct sarcastic arguments about them in one's head!

Couldn't we laugh about them instead? Or, simply note the difference, smile and let it go? Or, even better, see why someone might prefer their choices over mine!

Ronda:

Insights:

I tried changing my thoughts about some differences.

Instead of thinking about why I think skirts and dresses are more graceful than pants on women, I could think about how warm pants are in the winter. My friends in pants don't have to wear leg warmers under dresses as I do in the winter!

Instead of justifying being sedentary, I could plan to go on a walk, as my friend does, at least more often.

## Day 15: Accepting Difference

Instead of making fun of what seems like overly scrupulous re-cycling, I could make the tiny sacrifice of washing out the cat food cans for inclusion in the re-cycle bin. (from *Latest Journal 2023*)

Reader:

Insights: If this day's challenge resonates with you, write about some differences you need to accept and how you could think about them more lovingly.

## DAY 16: Forgiveness

From *A Healing of Memories* I wrote many years ago for my readers:

"Childhood: Thank you, God, for all the good memories of my childhood. Help me know that You were there cherishing me in my little ways and hopes, even when I felt lonely or passed over. If I was abused, sexually or emotionally, help me identify with You, Jesus, so unjustly treated in Your life on earth. Banish the demo of envy when I see other better loved in their childhoods who seem superior to me in some way… Forgive me for any catty, wild, or insensitive ways I treat others…"

"Adult: I call to memory times of trial where I felt disillusioned by the defects of friends, spouse, bosses, pastors. Give me the grace to forgive all these people as Yu have forgiven me for being a disappointment to them!"
(from *Taming the Lion Within: 5 Steps from Anger to Peace*, pp. 42-43)

Ronda:

Insights:

I made a list of all those people who hurt me greatly. Then I asked Jesus for the grace to forgive each one more intensely than in the past. I asked him to show me what each person was going through at the time he or she hurt me. It really helped me to forgive several people from the past much more totally!

Day 16: Forgiveness  35

Reader:

Insights: Think or write about what stands out for you about needing to forgive. Any specific people you need especially to forgive more?

# DAY 17: *Spiritual Friendship: Darkness and Light*

I wrote a whole little book entitled *Spiritual Friendship: Darkness and Light*. What is spiritual friendship? It is a relationship with another where the locus is loving the soul of the other and helping each other grow in holiness. Other friendships can be based on mutual love of some activity such as someone who also loves baseball. Or common life-style such as friends in a mother's group. In my book, I describe the stages in spiritual friendship: Attraction, Rejection or Mutuality, Enchantment, Union. Here is a prayer-poem I wrote about it:

"Are you real?
or did I invent you
 in my loneliness?
I touch the rough edges
and I rest secure."
(from *Prayer Poems*)

Ronda:

Insights: Now I look back and count some 12 friendships I would consider to be spiritual ones. Thank you God for the foretaste of heaven in the best times with those friends, especially the inspiration from knowing each of them. For the dark times I have repented of my part. Forgive me for ways I have disappointed any of them.

# Day 17: *Spiritual Friendship: Darkness and Light*

I rejoice in present spiritual friendships. I beg You, Jesus, to grace budding ones.

Reader:

Insights: Thank God for any spiritual friendships you have been graced to have.

# DAY 18: Popularity

Some of us were popular in the family, school, at work. But many of us were less than popular even rejected or bullied. In my case, in school, I was never popular with the majority. Even though I was pretty, I had protruding (then called buck) teeth, so I was not beautiful. But I was often the leader of the "out-group." As a professor I was popular with the students because I was an easy grader, but not popular with the other faculty since they resented my winning students by easy grades! The following was written for healing retreats for women, but I am using it here to apply to men as well as women:

"When we felt ourselves to be unpopular in school (or in the family, or at work) we were always popular with you, Jesus. We were the apple of your eye, for we were yours. (Not in the earthly sense where someone being popular excludes others being popular. You, dear God, are like good parents who love each child as if he/she were the only one.) Even if we didn't know you, God, (at one of those periods of our lives) you rejoiced in the knowledge that one day we would bask in your love as we may do from now on, if we choose." (*Freed to Love: Healing of Catholic Women*) p. 11.

If you are a male reader, you might want to frame this in the language more of approval as in realizing that God taps you on the head with praise for all the ways you try to do his will in the face of so many obstacles.

# Day 18: Popularity

Ronda:

Insights:

Why do I find it so hard to believe that I am popular with you, dear God? I am disappointed in myself not to be yet a saint. Still so many faults! However, you seem to be smiling at me as I write this and reassuring me. "Oh, dear Ronda, just as you love your pussycat even though she sometimes scratches and bites, I always love you!"

Reader:

Insights:

## DAY 19: Frustrations with Tech

Would anyone have thought that a man who was a horseback rider could learn to drive a car without any instructions?

So, why did we think that just because some of us were typists that we could do computer tech without taking lessons?

My son-in-law is a hard techie. My daughters became tech teachers and programmers. But I never have gotten beyond intermediate.

As a result, having never taken a course in tech, I have experienced about fifty years of frustration with tech!

I tried learning how to text, but after 8 little lessons by different friends, I gave up. I just can't stand the small keyboard so different from the old typewriters and the lap top keyboard.

But some of my friends and colleagues refuse to even do lap top. Some refuse to do e-mails. Some refuse to do voice-mail.

It is pretty hard to work with those old dinosaurs on projects! But, of course, others are thinking it is hard to work with Ronda who refuses to text. (*Latest Journal, 2023*)

Ronda:

Insights:

I want to take this opportunity to try once and for all to accept tech problems that I cannot solve myself.

# Day 19: Frustrations with Tech

Oh, Holy Spirit, I do believe that it is You who inspire inventors with new great machines. Thank you for everything I have been able, with help, to have done because of tech. When I get frustrated, please remind me to offer that up for graces for those I love, and alleviation of wider miseries of our times.

Reader:

Insights:

## DAY 20: Why Don't You Want to be My Friend?

In my book *The Way of Love*, the first segment is called What is Love and is about C.S. Lewis' concept of the Four Loves. They are: Passion, Familial Love, Friendship, and Charity.

Concerning friendship love, I liked to emphasize, as C. S. Lewis taught, that it is free. We are obligated to love family and help the needy, but we are not obligated to make a friend of a particular individual. Even if that person wants to be our friend.

How so? Friendship often begins with loving things in common all the way from baseball to God. But friendship is a gift from God.

St. Francis de Sales wrote that "people like you as much as God wants them to!"

There can be any reason, often trivial, why someone doesn't like you. Maybe you remind him of a bully in school because of the shape of your nose! Or, maybe this person has the first name of the most popular girl in school who didn't like you!

Ronda:

Insights:

Sometimes I have avoided a person who wanted to be my friend for some trivial reason, but then, since God wanted us to be friends, she wins me over!

With this in mind I want to forgive those in the past or present I wanted to be closer friends with but it didn't happen. Who knows what trait of mine this person didn't like! One I thought of immediately had a younger sister who was the family favorite and whose personality was a lot like mine!

And, thank You, profusely, God, for wanting so many wonderful people throughout my life to be my friend.

Reader:

Insights: Make a list of good friends you have had and thank God for each. Forgive anyone who didn't want to be your friend.

## DAY 21: "Our Hearts are Restless, until they find their Rest in Thee" (St. Augustine)

This famous quotation from the *Confessions* of St. Augustine has always been a favorite of mine.

However, the meaning of the word "restless" has changed for me over the decades.

Originally, I thought of restless as describing the result of all the things I tried that didn't work before I became a Catholic at age 21.

Later, it became more a matter of disappointment. "Oh, my husband wasn't the perfect character I thought he was?" "Oh, you mean angelic looking children aren't angelic?" "Oh, many students aren't eager to learn about Christian ethics, they are into sports and partying!" Oh, I am not a saint in spite of all my efforts."

So, restlessly I would dream of perfect people I might someday know or be…and reading Augustine's maxim helped me see that only God is perfect, only God is good and only in heaven will I be in total peace.

Ronda:

Insights:

Now, in the last decade of my life, restlessness often takes the form of impatience that I am still involved in daily life on earth. I wish, instead, I was already in heaven, or at least purgatory, where I will know at least that "I am home free." To such wishes Jesus always tells me "Surrender! You know not the day or the hour when I will come to fetch you!"

Reader:

Insights:

## DAY 22: How to Write Your Memoirs for Family and Friends

Back in the last century, I was running a writer's group in Sedona, Arizona where I was living with one of my daughters. A few of us were writing long books, but many wanted only to write short stories for their families to read one day.

I assembled these stories into a book called *The Fabric of our Lives.* The gimmick was to write about a piece of cloth that symbolized something big in your life such as a piece of your wedding gown or a swatch from your Navy uniform.

Here are some of the titles from the eventual 20 writers:

The Dolls Dress, The Blue and Gray Plaid Skirt, the Nightgown, the Lace Doily, my Brother's last Security Blanket.

You can order that book for postage-only at En Route Books and Media – https://www.enroutebooksandmedia.com.

Now, if you were thinking of writing such memories you could easily start with my first memory from childhood, what my parents were like, what my siblings were like, schooldays, romance, first job, best, job, mourning…etc.

Ronda:

Insights:

Some of my grandchildren, who don't necessarily love my big books, gave me and my twin-sister a gift called Storyworth with a hundred questions to spark the writing of memories for them to read. I found that little stories are different from big autobiographical works I have written. It amused me to write them and amused the readers.

Reader:

Insights: Consider writing your own memoirs in the form of short, short, stories. Maybe put one in here.

## DAY 23: "Humility is not thinking less of yourself but thinking of yourself less." C.S. Lewis

"How many sentences that you say begin with 'I'?" asked one of my spiritual directors! (see *Talkaholics*)

Now, it is only natural that much of our conversation oral or self-talk revolves around ourselves. We are the center only of our own selves and it is up to us alone to make tiny daily decisions such as when to wake up or when to brush one's teeth. At the same time, we realize that every other human being is also his or her own center of gravity. "Cada cabeza es un mondo" - each head is a world. Even more important we believe that God created each one of us out of love. We are so precious!

So, the first part of the title of this soundbyte – not to think less of oneself, is correct. On the other hand, true humility requires thinking of ourselves less…in the sense of obsessing over ones own needs and wants to the exclusion of the needs and wants of others around us! Talking incessantly about oneself is obviously not thinking of oneself less. We might try going through a day observing how often we are thinking and talking about ourselves in this excessive manner.

Ronda:

Insights:

I decided to spend a whole 24 hours, including times awaking up in the night, and turning thoughts about myself into prayer as in: Instead of thinking: "I

Day 23: "Humility is not thinking less of yourself but thinking of yourself less." - Lewis

am so afraid about what tomorrow will bring!" I can pray: "Dear Jesus, keep me from anxiety about the future. Help me to surrender it to You. Help me to serve others in love tomorrow."

Reader:

Insight:

## DAY 24: A Day of Giving Thanks

In my book *The Way of Love* I have a week of thanking God for everything. It is a favorite with all students and other readers.

Most of us thank God for beautiful sunsets, the stars, and beloved family members. That is good. But I have found that spending even a day thanking God for every tiny little thing changes the day from a time of grumbling about little frustrations to delighting in such tiny little things as:
toilet paper!

Ronda:

Insights:

Today, I made it a point to thank God for these gifts: How good that when it will snow tomorrow, I have a good warm house to stay in! How good that I just ate a wonderful vegetable soup with all those ingredients easily available at the supermarket without needing to plant and water things for months! How good that I have so many friends and acquaintances who want to talk to me in spite of all my defects.

# Day 24: A Day of Giving Thanks

Reader:

Insights: Write your own list.

## DAY 25: Learning from Pets?

I am relating this true story because those who have heard it find it so amusing:

"You're lonely living alone in that apartment, Mom? You've gotta get a cat."

"They charge a fee for pets. Forget it."

Months later my daughter, Diana, visits. "We have an appointment tomorrow to see this cat at The Cattery!"

Diana had seen this cat online.

I go into a lounge where this large residence for cats shows the ones that are for adoption. There are some 4 fat white cats, and one an striped orange one. The orange one was the one Diana had seen online.

I walked over and petted her. She immediately turned her head and bit me.

"Okay, forget about her," I decided.

The volunteer told me: "That one is not a cuddle-cat. She's a sassy cat."

"Ah, I thought, "sassy" is the euphemism for vicious!"

So I spent about 20 minutes staring at the cats in the lounge pondering this question:

"What's more important in life, cuddliness or beauty?"

Deciding on beauty, I went over to the orange one again and petted her. She accepted my gesture.

Because of these heavy thoughts that went into her selection I changed her name from Fawkes to Cleopatra.

So, one can learn from a pet!

# Day 25: Learning from Pets?

Ronda:

Insights:

A much more important insight I got from Cleopatra after years of companionship is this: We can wonder how the absolute God can love us tiny little humans. There is an abyss between God and us. However, consider, even though there is an abyss between a human and a cat, I have no trouble loving her, even when she sometimes bites and scratches. If I am merciful, shouldn't I count on the mercy of God for me?

Reader:

Insights:

# DAY 26: Joy at Holy Mass

Many traditional Catholics who love the old Latin Mass like to emphasize the good that it does for the soul to be silent before Mass. They object to how some Catholics at the English Mass chat before Mass and even talk during Mass.

I do appreciate silence before Holy Mass as a help to becoming recollected. At the same time, I like to ask also about joy. How is it that at most Holy Masses even if the readings are about joy in the Lord, the congregation looks as if they were at a funeral?

In response, traditional Catholics sometimes reply that they experience joy in the heart, though not expressed by smiles or lifting the hands in praise.

To this, I respond – so if someone chatting before Mass says they experience reverence in the heart even though they are talking, would you accept that?

(About Joy in prayers see, *Why I am a Catholic Charismatic*)

Ronda:

Insights:

When I got the graces of charismatic gifts way back in 1969, I loved the joyful praise at the meetings. My twin-sister, Carla De Sola, the sacred dancer, expresses and encourages such joy by leading congregations in joyful movement. I always find that singing joyful songs loudly and moving joyfully lifts my heart to God.

# Day 26: Joy at Holy Mass

Reader:

Insights: How do you express joy in God in your Church life?

# DAY 27: Live in the Now

This spiritual advice became popular toward the end of the 20$^{th}$ century, partly influenced, I think, by Zen Buddhism. In my Philosophy of Time courses I would give the students a questionnaire to see if they predominantly Lived in the Past, Lived in the Future, of Lived in the Present – the "now."

Since I tend to think of the past and the present as heavy with big and small sufferings, I always test out as trying to live in the future. How? By means of fantasies of utopian living, work, and ministry situations.

So, what's so bad about that?

First, there is no utopia on earth. As one mentor put it "every utopia becomes a gulag."

Second, it takes time and energy away from enjoying or improving the present.

Ronda:

Insights:

Trying to live in the now I forced myself to pray to accept what the now is offering me and describing to myself the good in the now such as:

> the beauty of the falling snow today;
> the joy that there is a TV Mass when I can't get to the Church because of the snow;

# Day 27: Live in the Now

the comfortable feeling of my joyful other dedicated widow watching that TV Mass right next to me on the lap-top;

the anticipation of a delicious lunch of pork roast from last night's dinner…

Reader:

Insights: See if you are more inclined to the past, the future or the now. Jot down your "now" blessings.

## DAY 28: There is an Abyss between an Ardent Catholic and a Saint

So taught Dietrich Von Hildebrand. Since he was an extremely ardent Catholic, but not, I thought, a saint, I found this idea fascinating. However, in the last years of his life when he was suffering painfully in retirement I did think he became holy. So what is that huge difference?

I wrote many books about the saints, and one of the ways I define sanctity is that the woman or man is so close to Christ that she or he wants to suffer with him. By contrast, an ardent Catholic accepts the sufferings that come without complaint but prays to be free of any that are possible. In my book *The Way of Love*, I define saintliness as having nothing but love in one's heart. Not having love in the "largest part" of one's heart but also pockets of the bad kind of anger, or despair, self-pity, or simply "blahs."

Once I was reading a book about St. Catherine of Siena and I told my spiritual director that he had a great challenge. He had to make me into St. Catherine. He replied: 'God has St. Catherine. He wants St. Ronda.' So, I ask myself, given my God given personality, what would I be like as a saint?

Ronda:

Insights:

I pray that this day Jesus would give me the grace to be holy. For this time of my life that seems to me to be:

- being gentle, patient, and peaceful in every interaction with others;

# Day 28: There is an Abyss between an Ardent Catholic and a Saint

- not dwelling on past sins and faults but hopeful because 'with God all things are possible';
- immediately lifting my anxieties for the future into the loving hearts of Jesus, Mary and Joseph.

Talking to Al, my spiritual director, about a 'fleece' I was thinking about, he had this so insightful advice: "Putting down "fleeces" is abrogating responsibility for our own decisions. As if I can manipulate God to send me a particular sign, and remove all responsibility for making my own decision.

Cat and abyss: "I hope that these lectures will make it possible for you to laugh at your paltry conflicts, to smile at your fear of not being right, and to joke at your urge to prove others wrong. If you manage to do that your conflicts, fears and apprehensions will be relieved, and the recovered patient will return to a home pervaded by the spirit of patience and forbearance and a sense of humor." *Peace versus Power in the Family, p. 84*

Worst defect from *Way of Love*—Love and Admire but not follow: "Hate the sin, love the sinner," St. Augustine famously wrote. So, we might rightly judge that in a difference with us, the other person is wrong, and yet accept that she or he believes something out of value blindness. In many cases we can still be friends. But not if I think I must pound into the other person's head why she or he is wrong. I can speak the truth with love sometimes but accept the difference.

Reader:

Insight:

## DAY 29: DISLIKE OF CHANGE

"When you tire of living, change itself seems evil…for then any change at all disturbs the deathlike peace of the life-weary!" (From Walter M. Miller, Jr.'s book *A Canticle for Liebowitz* – an old abbot says to himself on p. 138 – saved in my *Latest Journal 2022*)

As I write these Soundbytes I am 85 years old and identify very much with this strange quotation!

Any change, even for the good, such as an invitation to a dinner out breaks my usual rhythm of daily life. How much more the prospect of moving to a new living situation in a different State!

I am not weary of life because it doesn't include wonderful memories of life with my beloved family, or joy in the times as a professor and speaker where the words I think the Holy Spirit inspired me to say, actually changed people's lives. I never weary of Holy Mass or of good times with those I am presently living with as a Dedicated Widow.

It is more daily life that wearies me with all the petty particulars: now brush your teeth, now rinse the dishes, now get dressed. Yet that rhythm, being the norm, is lulling and so changes are disturbing.

Ronda:

Insights:

Pondering all of this prayerfully, I seem to hear the Holy Spirit speaking to me in this way:

# Day 29: Dislike of Change

"Beware of angelism!"

(Angelism is when humans wish they were like angels without bodies, pure spirits. It is wrong because it is a refusal of the gift of the soul/body composite God chose for each of us humans.)

"God wants you to work out your salvation is an embodied person. Would you want your adorable pussy-cat to be a picture of a cat (the idea of catness) instead of the embodied furry little creature she was created to be?"

"So offer up the sufferings of daily life and be thankful for the joys and humbly await "the new heaven and the new earth" that will be yours in eternity."

Reader:

Insight:

## DAY 30: Why go to Confession?

Some wonder why anyone has to go to Confession to a priest rather than simply ask Jesus for forgiveness directly. In my very first book *The Church of Love* I use these words to explain:

"Using the analogy of human love, we can go more deeply into the logic attending contrition and forgiveness. When two people are in love, every sensibility in them is heightened. A person previously smug and self-satisfied finds himself full of sorrow when he sees how his thoughtless actions have wounded his loved one…rather than let the woman he loves think that he doesn't care, or that he will never change, he rushes eagerly to say that he is sorry. He doesn't just feel sorry…he needs to know that she accepts his sorrow and, most of all that his act did not destroy the bond of love irrevocably. The spoken words, 'I forgive you' are the seal of this reunion…

"In sin, we turn away from trust in Christ's love and providence in favor of frantically chasing what we think to be our happiness. For example, when one despairs that God really cares about one's future and will send the needed love one tends to embrace fleeting pleasures. In fact, since Christ continually offer us love and guarantees our final happiness, it is a rejection of this love when we try to grab it for ourselves contrary to his will...

"Sorrow for sin seeks a definite verbal expression…The grace (divine love) in the words of absolution and the deeds of penance reseal the bond between I and Thou."

This book, *The Church of Love*, has been excerpted by the Magnificat magazine for many years.

# Day 30: Why go to Confession?

Ronda:

Insight:

Sorrowfully, I have to go to Confession about once a month minimum, almost always for venial sins of anger. I always feel strengthened to continue struggling with God's grace after receiving the sacrament. After face to face confession became available after Vatican II, I found that I loved seeing the mercy of God in the face of the priest. You might think: "Well, Ronda, if you still got angry, why do you think the sacrament works?" To which I sometimes reply humorously, "You should be glad I go. Otherwise I might murder uou!"

There was a priest I knew who heard confessions at daily Mass in a warm Church without air-conditioning. I was praising him for his sacrifice. How memorable was his response:

"I love hearing confessions because of the sincerity and humility of those confessing."

Reader:

Insight:

## DAY 31: How Photo Collections on the Lap-top Screen Bring Joy

Those of you who know me personally certainly know that I usually find tech frustrating. However, one aspect of it that I absolutely love is my Screen-Saver Photos. My collection that parades across the screen 24/7 includes those techies helped me put up for decades and also the whole collections of my daughters – both techies, by the way. I like to joke that when people are having their photos taken they smile, so even family and friends who might not smile at me all the time, on the screen saver seem to be delighted to see me!

> "Lookie, lookie, Ronda, there's you and your twin at 1 years old surrounded by your father and mother looking at you with so much love!"
> "Lookie, lookie, Ronda, there's you and your fiancé being married in a Church in Rome way back in 1961!"
> "Lookie, lookie, Ronda, there are photo of the children who died as adults smiling with joy."
> "Lookie, lookie, Ronda, there is you with your hand on the back of St. John Paul II at that audience. And there's you with Mother Angelica."

Ronda:

Insight:

Thanksgiving is the greatest remedy for anxiety or depression. Why not have a revolving screen saver on your phone or lap-top with all those moments saved and bringing you fresh joy?

Day 31: How Photo Collections on the Lap-top Screen Bring Joy

Reader:

Insights:

(from *Latest Journal, 2023*)

# DAY 32: Looking Forward to Your Resurrected Body

One of my jokes when giving talks with many elderly women present is this:
"When you look in the mirror don't think 'every day I look less and less like Marilyn Monroe.' Say, instead, 'every day in every way I look more like Mother Teresa.' A masculine form could be don't think you look less like Clark Gable, but more like St. Augustine.

I have found it helpful to imagine each day, thankfully, what my resurrected body will be like. In the book *What the Saints Said about Heaven,* my co-authors, Richard Ballard and Ruth Ballard, included a chapter about the resurrected body. See also (*What Now?: A Roadmap for 80 Year Olds and Beyond*, co-author Al Hughes)

Summarizing the teachings of the Church culled from Scripture, theology, and the writings of the saints, we can anticipate that should we have the grace to reach heaven, at the final Day of Judgment we will receive our resurrected bodies. These bodies will be:

Youthful
Agile (swift as thought)
Perfect
Immortal
Glorified
Pain-free
Bright-Shining
Seeing God 'face to face'

# Day 32: Looking Forward to Your Resurrected Body

Ronda:

Insights:

Because I was always a 'klutz' (clumsy oaf) and my non-identical twin-sister was a beautiful, graceful sacred dancer, whenever I think of my resurrected body I imagine myself dancing.

How good for me it would be if whenever I am in pain, or simply tired out, or looking in the mirror, I would imagine my resurrected body!

Guardian angel mine, remind me to do so!

Reader:

Insights:

## DAY 33: How Our Relationship to Our Parents and Family can affect Our Relationship to God, Our Father, and to Mary, Our Mother.

Many years ago I co-authored these books: *Bringing the Mother with You: Healing Meditations on the Mysteries of the Rosary* and *How Shall we Find the Father* – co-authors Sister Mary Neill and Don Briel)

Helpful to ourselves and our readers were the theories we explored about how some of us project onto God the Father and Mary our Mother the qualities of our original relationship to our parents (birth, adoptive, or care-givers).

How so? My father left when we were 8 years old. Besides that, when he was with us, he was very factual vs. affectionate. Always teaching us, since he had a kind of encyclopedic mind. My co-authors had an exercise they gave where you write down all the characteristics of your human father and then see how many of those you always think of God the Father as having.

When I converted from atheism, I fell in love with Christ, the savior of my soul, but the God the Father seemed to me to be distant. Absolute wisdom, but not over-flowing love!

Then, with Mary, since my mother was warm but highly critical, I tend to love Mary, but always think she is disapproving of me!

Remedies? A help has been praying to God the Father while breathing deeply: Abba, Father, Abba Father, Abba Father…

The Hebrew word "Abba" reminds me of warm Jewish men.

With Mother Mary? I'm not sure…I will try now to find a remedy.

Ronda:

Insights:

    I am remembering how many decades ago Mary changed my life. Some devout women from the parish brought to my home the Pilgrim Statue of Our Lady of Fatima to keep for a few weeks. There was a consecration prayer where we prayed that Mary would take our hearts and place her own heart in us. I said the prayer without any thought. Immediately, I received tremendous contem-plative graces from the Holy Trinity. This lasted for many years. I realized that I had not understood the contemplative side of Mary, viewing her only as an intercessor.

    Now, recalling those graces, I come to you, dear, dear, Mother Mary. I see that your love for us takes the form always of bringing us closer to your beloved Son. Was it also you, dear widow Mary, who helped inspire me to want to be a Dedicated Widow of Jesus? Yes!!!!!

Reader:

Insight: (is there anything from the above that you want to bring to prayer?)

## DAY 34: Padre Pio's Healing Prayer

(from my *Latest Journal, 2023*)

Heavenly Father, I thank you for loving me.
I thank you for sending your Son, Our Lord Jesus Christ,
to the world to save and to set me free.
I trust in your power and grace that sustain and restore me.
Loving Father, touch me now with your healing hands,
for I believe that your will is for me to be well in mind, body, soul and spirit.
Cover me with the most precious blood of your Son,
our Lord, Jesus Christ from the top of my head to the soles of my feet.
Cast anything that should not be in me.
Root out any unhealthy and abnormal cells.
Open any blocked arteries or veins and rebuild and replenish any damaged areas.
Remove all inflammation and cleanse any infection
by the power of Jesus' precious blood.
Let the fire of your healing love pass through my entire body
to heal and make new any diseased areas
so that my body will function the way you created it to function.
Touch also my mind and my emotion, even the deepest recesses of my heart.
Saturate my entire being with your presence, love, joy and peace
and draw me ever closer to you every moment of my life.
And Father, fill me with your Holy Spirit and empower me to do your work
so that my life will bring glory and honor to your holy name.
I ask this in the name of the Lord Jesus Christ.
Amen.

# Day 34: Padre Pio's Healing Prayer

This healing prayer clearly stands by itself. I brought into it those with terrible crosses of pain.

Ronda:

Insights:

I need to stop complaining about small infirmities. At present I don't have any big ones, thanks be to God. I need especially to pray for healing of the types of emotions evident in useless anxieties.

Reader:

Insights:

## DAY 35: Excuses for Abortion

(taken from *Living in Love: About Christian Ethics*, now in print as part of the *Way of Love*.)

Most if not all of the readers of this book will be among those convinced that destroying innocent babies in the womb is a terrible thing. I taught this subject in ethics classes with undergrads and seminarians for many decades.

It seemed to help readers to go through my reasoning about how to refute typical excuses made for having abortions. I concocted a romance between 2 pre-med college students and the thinking that might tempt them. To my great surprise, there was a student in one of my classes who was often yelling out 4 letter words at me. At the end of the class she confessed that these dialogues exactly used the words that she, herself, had said to herself to justify having an abortion. My class seemed to have made a dent in her mentality.

Excuse I - I've Gotta Survive.

Excuse II - My Conscience Doesn't Bother Me.

Excuse III - It's for the Greater Good. Nobody will be Hurt.

Excuse IV - Everybody's Doing It.

Excuse V - Nobody's Perfect, I'm not a Saint.

If you are curious as to how I refuted each of these, get the original book, *Living in Love*, or the big book *The Way of Love*.

# Day 35: Excuses for Abortion

Ronda:

Insights:

Bringing up children myself I realize it's a 24-hour responsibility. Absolutely worth it. Still it is easy to understand that in our present-day culture many women will feel overwhelmed over a pregnancy that they did not plan for. The above excuses will seem to many self-evident reasons to abort the child. How important it is that so many pro-lifers not only pray in front of abortion clinics and try to talk women out of the wrong decision, but also give them immediate access of services that offer adoption or years of financial support and living situations. Meetings offering healing from abortion help many women to move forward. For some 40 years in different cities I prayed in front of abortion clinics once a week with inter-faith groups of other pro-lifers. What joy when a woman listened to alternatives and saved her baby!

Reader:

Insights:

## DAY 36: The Child is the Love of the Parents made Visible

This teaching of Dietrich Von Hildebrand in his classic *Marriage* I have found to intrigue everyone I ever tell it to.

I think it refers not only to physical traits inherited in the case of biological parenthood, but also to other traits. For example, my daughter, Carla, and my son Charlie, both looked more like me, I always thought, and Diana more like my husband, Martin. Now Carla and Diana are identical twins but their facial expressions made them look different.

So, since I loved my husband's face and whole body, I liked to see aspects of it in the children, including my daughters becoming even rounder in middle age. And, he liked to see my darker hair, brown vs. blue eyes, in our daughters.

Also I loved to see my husband's deep literary mind reflected in our children's written words. I think he liked to see in them great talkativeness even though he was much more a lover of silence. I loved that my husband's great enjoyment of music was reflected in our son becoming a cellist and a composer. (See Music of Charles Chervin on the web).

Ronda:

Insights:

Thank you, dear God, for creating those so beloved children of ours. Sometimes when I was upset with certain characteristics of my husband, I would think:

"Yes, but, if I had married someone better about that aspect, I wouldn't have had those specific marvellous children.

It was a revelation to me when I first found out that babies aren't individual souls put in any body any time but in the specific genetically-coded body created by that specific sperm and egg.

Reader:

Insights: (if you are a single person, you might think and/or write about couples and their children you have loved).

## DAY 37: Passive Purification

The term "passive purification" is most often found in Carmelite spirituality. The idea is that we imagine we will get closer to God by actively exercising more will-power to overcome our sins, faults, and defects. We certainly need to will to be freed from them. However, most often more freedom from that tyranny comes not from will-power or even insight, but from the acceptance of the crosses in life.

These crosses are permitted by God and designed by Him to purify us of desires and pride that are obstacles to union with God – to the holiness we long for. A key example would be when sexual sins lead to horrible sometimes even deadly diseases. Bankruptcy from over-spending would be another example. Less extreme or tragic can be such set-backs as finding that talking too much about oneself in a self-centered manner has alienated a treasured friend! Over-eating can lead to pain in the legs. We beg God for insight and for greater will-power, often granted, but more powerful can be the blow to our vices that come from such passive (unwilled) purifications.

(See *Spirituality for all Times: Readings from the Catholic Classics,* co-author: Kathleen Brouillette)

Ronda:

Insights:

A present-day passive purification I am undergoing as I write these Soundbytes is waiting to try out a greatly-desired living situation for a good

## Day 37: Passive Purification

year when I thought I would only have a month's wait. Potentially this cross can free me from a tendency to picture future homes as utopian. But all the saints insist that only heaven is perfect and everything on earth is limited.

When I bring the cross of waiting to Jesus in prayer, He sometimes tells me such truths as this one: 'It doesn't matter where you live. What matters is to be closer to Me!' Or, opening myself to Him in deep breathing prayer, I simply feel less anxious and more peaceful.

Reader:

Insights: (Reread the soundbyte slowly to see if there is some message for you in it.)

## DAY 38: Everlasting or Eternal?

Some Christians are puzzled about what eternal life will be like. We cannot know as St. Paul said so eloquently. But we can have some idea and some glimpses. Many decades ago I wrote an article about the meaning of the word "eternal." I distinguish between these two definitions: 'Time without End' and 'Timelessness'.

Everlastingness is time without end. That means that there is no end to time. Everlasting beings include all those creatures who begin in time including angels and humans, but who don't have a final moment…we keep going in one form or another. For humans, we keep going from body/soul composites to pure souls, to our resurrected body/soul composite. And we grow from glory to glory. Or, of course, if we are in hell from misery to misery.

Timelessness is the state of being of God. God is unchanging, absolute being. God always was, and has no beginning and no end. You might ask: Isn't Scripture full of passages about God changing His mind? This is how I think about this puzzle. I imagine a large dot at the top of a page and then rays coming out of the dot going down to the bottom of the page at angles. There is a line at the bottom of the page. We move along the bottom of the page and our deeds go up toward the dot at the top. God at the top is timeless being, but all the rays of what goes on in time go up toward him. What to us is moment by moment in time is crystallized in one moment which is timeless.

So, Scripture, designed for us who are in time, describes God's ways as changing in response to our good deeds or vices, but in Him it is all in the timelessness of His perfect justice and mercy. Now eternal in the sense of timelessness is impossible for us to imagine. The best way I find to try to ima-

# Day 38: Everlasting or Eternal?

gine eternal in the sense of timelessness is to recall extremely joyful moments where time seemed to have stood still. When I ask students or those in an audience to give examples they usually talk about seeing a baby of theirs for the first time, or about viewing a spectacular sunset.

Ronda:

Insights:

I am so used to everlasting time in the form of the minute by minute process of getting through each day and night of my long, long, life! I long for the eternity of joy in God, participating in God's timelessness in some mysterious way. Though always myself will be only everlasting, not eternal in the timeless sense. Yet I am so used to living moment by moment, that in quiet prayer it is hard to simply let God immerse me in His timeless love and beauty. If asked: "Do you want to come to Me right now to participate in my timeless goodness?" I would certainly say "Yes." The obstacle is that I am afraid of purgatory, purported to be a much greater suffering than anything we experience on earth.

No remedy I can see. Only "I surrender, dear creator God, to live in how ever much time on earth You decree. Increase my love for my eternity with You so much that I accept every suffering necessary to purify my soul."

Reader:

Insights:

## DAY 39: Becoming a Dedicated Widow

After my husband left this earth when I was 57 years old, I hoped to find a perfect saintly second husband. Some 12 single men rejected me. I joked years afterwards that men of 70 years old who never married, it wasn't because they hadn't met me! Thinking that Jesus would not reject me, I wanted to become a consecrated widow. This vocation, though the first consecration in the early Church, is being experimented with in the Church at this time. I tried to interest various Bishops to accept me in this role, but when none expressed interest, my spiritual director suggested I call myself a Dedicated Widow with a similar rule of life. This required only the permission of a priest.

In the meantime, I had written a book about widow saints called *A Widow's Walk: Encouragement, Comfort and Wisdom from the Widow Saints.* (a revised version helpful for grief-ministry was printed later under the title *Walk with me Jesus: A Widow's Journey* – this version includes a Stations of the Cross for Widows I wrote.) My basic rule of life as a Dedicated Widow was to take Jesus as my Bridegroom, never to re-marry, go to Daily Mass, pray the Rosary, the Mercy Chaplet, Morning Prayer, Evening Prayer and Night Prayer, with two period of silent prayer as well. I would dress in simple blue denim, or other cheap fabrics, that I could buy at the Thrift-shop. In this way, I can give as much as possible to the poor from my income as a Catholic philosophy professor, then, and later less from my pension and social security when I retired. I have loved this vocation for several decades. A few other widows also call themselves dedicated widows, each with her own rule of life.

On the humorous side, my husband, before he left this world asked me what I would do when he died. I said I would become a nun. He joked: "You can't become a nun?" "Why not?" "Because you *are* a nun." I laughed and laughed. He didn't mean it as a compliment.

My daughter, Diana, when I started wearing my simple blue denim outfits with a blue kerchief on me head, made this crack. I asked her to walk me to the store when I was visiting her. She said: "I won't go with you. I don't want to look like the illegitimate child of a monk-ess!"

(See my little book *The Comic Catholic* for more jokes, general and family.)

Ronda:

Insights:

The part of being a dedicated widow that is probably hardest for me is to really believe that Jesus wants to be my bridegroom in spite of all my defects of character. It consoles me a little to realize that so great a saint as Teresa of Avila always thought of herself as a miserable sinner even though she was so clearly chosen to be one of the greatest of those consecrated women beloved of Christ. And wouldn't I be a beloved bride of Jesus as a dedicated widow even if I didn't reach sainthood? Finally, as a life-long teacher, I come back to the idea that even if I got a "D" for conduct, always confessing my sins, I would still get an "A" for effort! To this Jesus seemed to respond: "Dear little Ronda, I try to free you from those defects, indeed, but I never reject your precious selfhood."

Reader:

Insights: (whatever you vocation is, write about it here.)

## DAY 40: "You can only love yourself, loving."

This is a quotation from Thomas Aquinas, little known. At first sight it isn't that clear but once I got it, I loved it and included it in my book *The Way of Love.*

Here is how I understand it. We are ordered by Jesus to love others as we love ourselves. However, most of us don't love ourselves very much, so what does that mean?

I believe that Jesus meant that we are to care for their needs the way we care for our own needs.

We can't love ourselves, however, when we are being unloving. Examples:

I am thinking nasty thoughts about someone who hurt or annoyed me. If I happen to look in a mirror I will see my face full of angry disgruntlement.

But, now consider that I am thinking loving thoughts about someone who has helped or delighted me, or forgiving thoughts about someone who hurt me. If I happen to look in the mirror or at my face on a zoom, it will be my best face. And, then, I can love myself loving!

Think about it!

Ronda:

Insights:

Right now my big challenge to love myself is that my mind is teeming with anxious thoughts. Even though I can find many reasons to try to justify anxiety, of course, that is contrary to Jesus telling us not to fear but to trust in

Him. My co-author, Al Hughes, a counselor and spiritual director, wrote a whole book about escaping anxiety. See *Escaping Anxiety Along the Road to Spiritual Joy*.

So, Jesus, I surrender all that anxiety to you. Flood my mind with trust in You.

Reader:

Insights:

## DAY 41: Can we be Joyful even in the Midst of Tragedy?

"Rejoice in the Lord, always, again I say Rejoice." (Philippians 4:4-9)

The Lutheran theologian Soren Kierkegaard taught this interesting thing about the above passage from Scripture:

Between the first 'rejoice' and the second 'rejoice', we might think of all the reasons we are not rejoicing and then, by the second 'rejoice', about why we need to rejoice just the same.

Very often I find someone talks about all those who are suffering today. Pray for them. I am critical about this because it seems to me most of us suffer every day in one form or another.

Huge example? Did Jesus only suffer during the night before the Crucifixion, and the Passion itself? Didn't He suffer every day of His life, seeing the sin around Him and the pain it caused?

Besides don't we all suffer every day from the frustrations of daily life, from thoughts of the evils around us such as babies being slaughtered in the womb perhaps only 5 miles away?

So what are those reasons to rejoice after we have considered all the suffering, personal or around us?

Ronda:

Insights:

It give me joy simply to enumerate these joys!

# Day 41: Can we be Joyful even in the Midst of Tragedy?

First, the existence of God: all Good, all Powerful, all Knowing, all Just, Merciful…total LOVE.

Second, that God's Son, Jesus the Christ, has opened for us the possibility of an eternity of happiness if we follow Him, and repent when we haven't followed Him.

Third, that God created us, and all those we love.

Fourth, the Holy Bible.

Fifth, the beauty of nature around us – even a flower growing on the patch of ground in a city slum.

Sixth, the beauty of music, art, dance, literature, film.

Seventh, specific personal gifts, such as food, clothing, housing.

Reader:

Insights:

## DAY 42: Will what you are about to say help me to love this person?

"Let no corrupt word proceed out of your mouth, but what is good for necessary edification, that it may impart grace to the hearers." (Ephesians 4:29)

Many years ago my twin-sister had an unusual mentor: Paul Leahy was his name, later part of the L'Arche group homes. (In case you might need to know, this world-wide movement provides homes for the developmentally disabled to live with others understood to be less intellectually disabled but often less good at love of God and neighbor!)

Paul used to startle us. For example, once coming for dinner, he asked that I bring out a basin and he began to wash all of our feet!

A challenge he posed for loquacious, gossipy, me, was that when I began to tell some story about someone I knew he would gently ask:

"So, Ronda, is what you are about to say going to help me love this person more?"

Most of the time it wasn't.

In fact, it was only many decades after he left the scene that I happened upon the sin of detraction on a list for Lenten examination of conscience. In my booklet entitled *Talkaholics*, I refer to this malady. Calumny is when we lie about someone to get them in trouble. That I have never done. But detraction is telling the truth, but for no reason but the fun of telling an interesting story or the fun of ridicule.

Now there can be a good reason to tell a bad truth about another. We should warn our children about friendship with those who can lead them into sin.

I wonder! If I kept a scorecard for a week of how many stories I tell about the edifying good others do or say, compared to the number of stories about the bad they do or say, which list would be the longest?

Ronda:

Insight:

To avoid the sin of detraction, I like to figure out 'pastoral reasons' for the juicy gossip. For example, I am only telling you about this sin of so and so in order to encourage you to pray for him or her.

Please guardian angel mine, put a gag over my mouth and let me always first pray before telling tales to see if it will really be edifying to tell a particular memory about that person.

Reader:

Insights:

## DAY 43: Personality Types – Helpful or Harmful?

In the 1970's many of us got into personality tests such as Myers-Briggs, the Enneagram, and the 4 Temperaments. I found them helpful for self-understanding but also for better tolerance of those of opposite types.

I test out as a high extrovert on Myers-Briggs, but my husband was an introvert. Extroverts typically love to be around other people and get energy from self-expression in words. But introverts, even if they are friendly, get energy more from being alone. For our marriage to be better I had to accept that it was as hard for him to have me talk at him from earliest AM as it was for me to deal with his long silences.

Even harder is that I am an extremely orderly person, liking to plan weeks ahead ever hour of the day, whereas everyone else in my immediate family are the play it by ear flexible type. On the Enneagram, I test out as a "1" – the crusader type always trying to win in battles against evils large and small. I am told that I do better if I go to my next over "2" helper type or to the "4" creative type. On the 4 temperaments I am choleric vs. phlegmatic, and sanguine if I am in control but very melancholic if others are in control!

Some mentors of mine have become disgusted with these personality tests. Some dub them as psycho-babble. Others insist that labelling those different from oneself in this way is a form of rejection. And telling others all day that I am this type or that is a way to justify bad behavior. You will find reference to these types throughout all of my journals.

Many traditional Catholics associate personality typologies with progressive theology. Yet, there were some Catholic psychiatrists and psychologists, most prominently Karl Stern, and Fr. Benedict Groeschel who used

# Day 43: Personality Types – Helpful or Harmful?

psychological insights a great deal as a help in spirituality, if not specifically being into the personality typologies.

Ronda:

Insights:

My inclination is to run with the typologies as a help to understanding myself and others in daily life. At the same time, I need to be aware of those criticisms and avoid falling into the negatives of labeling. Especially I must not use them as excuses for any wrong choices or attitudes. For example, just because being a super-planner is a gift for getting a lot done that is good, I need not be rigid about the timing of small conflicts in daily life. What is the most loving way to think or act in this situation needs to prevail over clinging to what suits me best.

Reader:

Insights:

## DAY 44: Called by Name: Following a Personal Spirituality

I wrote a book by that title many years ago. It is free on En Route Books and Media. Here is a quotation:

"I believe that there are other ardent Catholics like me who just don't fit into one of those well-trodden paths such as Benedictine, Franciscan, Dominican, Carmelite…devotional, Charismatic Covenant Community, Opus Dei…

"I don't want to define myself as an eccentric loner. I want to follow a personal spirituality that includes all that I love in the traditional ways – that is somehow *my* way but also part of *our* way."

The chapters in the book include: God's Way. No Way, My Way, Their Way, Your Way, Our Way…Home Free!

Since the little book is available for free on En Route Books and Media…here I simply want to refer to a few ideas that could interest you.

God's way is that spirituality that will bring us into union with Himself, obeying what Jesus taught about what real goodness is. But we will be different than St. John, for instance, because we live in our century, in our moment in time with our own personalities.

We can feel at an impasse if we try to be like some admired saint or mentor in ways that don't fit our own gifts. I love to read about contemplatives, but I am a very active person. So I don't become more spiritual by spending many more hours in prayer. Still I can never be too active to have good times each day of quiet prayer.

An example of spontaneity in personal spirituality was St. John Paul II. He was a dramatist before he became a philosopher/theologian/priest. An instant

# Day 44: Called by Name: Following a Personal Spirituality

I love is that he was addressing as Pope a big youth group. Seeing that they looked restless and bored, he suddenly turned his fingers over into seeming eye-glasses and laughed at them. I knew a teen who was totally converted back to the Catholic faith because of going to such a youth rally of John Paul II!

The little book tells of spiritualities that are not mine but "theirs." The way of service, the way of peace, the way of trust. At different times in my life some of these could be beckoning.

Ronda:

Insight:

Amusingly enough, I will say, at this point a big part of my spirituality is SOUNDBYTES. That is, mixing with others in Church or at gatherings or even with a cashier at a grocery story and saying something provocative in a loving manner.

At an airport, seeing a young black couple with wonderful hair-do's and colorful loose African style clothing sitting waiting for our flight, I walked up to them. "I just want to tell you that I love the way you look." They seemed delighted.

Reader:

Insights:

## DAY 45: "Now and at the hour of our death"

How many times do most of us pray those words at the end of the Hail Mary? My god-father, Balduin Schwarz, the philosopher, used to teach that these famous words signify:

> The past is gone, the future is not yet,
> so the only times that really count for us are
> NOW and the HOUR OF OUR DEATH!!!

This doesn't mean that the past wasn't real or that we don't need to plan prudently for the future. It means that we should not live in the past or the future in a way that impedes our experiencing the graces of the present moment and our longing for the total fulfillment that will be ours in heaven one day if we follow our Lord.

Ronda:

Insights:

I pray the Hail Mary, about 50 times a day. Dear Mother Mary, help me to become more conscious that you are praying for me, a sinner, so many times a day at least! Thank you, dear mother Mary, for your love and help.

Marti Armstrong, the Dedicated Widow, read this and sighed. "Yes, we need to see the bright colors of the present."

Day 45: "Now and at the hour of our death"

Reader:

Insight:

## DAY 46: Recovery International for Anger, Anxiety, and Depression

In my book *Taming the Lion Within: 5 Steps from Anger to Peace*, I wrote about the terrific program devised by Abraham Low before the more famous 12 Step Anonymous group for addicts.

I became involved in the 1990's. Anger was what I confessed to the most often. A priest suggested I try to look into psychological aspects that might be underlying my sins.

Going to group meetings for some 30 years brought me from 5 fits a day to 2 explosions a week!

The program involves applying "tools" to everyday life situations of anger, anxiety and depression. Here are some of my favorites, described in more detail in *Taming the Lion*.

Here I will only give an example of each:

*Take a Secure Thought* – I am late for an important meeting. Instead of panicking and blaming others, I could think "I can call up and tell them what I would have said at the meeting."

*Accept the Average* – A wife is angry because her husband comes home and doesn't want to hear about her day. Instead of pouting, she could remember that it is average for him to be tired after a long day of work and the commute and wait until after the children are in bed to talk to him.

>   *Move your Muscles* – when feeling anxious or depressed it is good to move about – if not taking a walk, even doing some physical task vs. sitting around brooding.
>
>   *Humor is your Best Friend* – any time you can joke about something you feel less angry.

If you identify with any of the above search on the web for Recovery International. There are person to person meetings but also online and phone meetings. No fee, no commitment. You can just try.

Ronda:

Insights:

Even though this program is not Christian or even religious as such, the common sense tools work against the pride Jesus tries to overcome. Common-sense is humble whereas "my way or the highway," is not!

Reader:

Insights:

## DAY 47: Games: Silly or Good?

Since I was hoping that by age 85 that I would be levitating on the ceiling in holy rapture, I was surprised that in retirement I had lots of free time.

In some of the places I lived in my 80's lots of elders played games. Since as a child I loved games such as solitaire, monopoly, and then later scrabble, I thought I would try playing games again. Enjoying the games and the lighter fellowship with others they provided, I wondered about them. It seemed to me that one of the good aspects of playing games is that they are meaningless!

In times full of personal, world-wide, and Church crises, that are so, so, serious, didn't it feel good to do something meaningless? I jumped on the fact that playing games is supposed to be good for the mind, to postpone dementia.

Now, at the Assisted Living place I was in for almost a year, some of the residents spent up to 6 hours a day playing games. For me, still writing little books and, even more important, going to Holy Mass and praying for a total of some 3-4 hours a day, with 3 hours a day eating in the dining room, certainly I would not want to play games in all the remaining hours.

My present 2 hours a day at most for games takes the form of playing our own version of triple solitaire with my house-mates. The good part is that we get a break from the kind of petty conflicts of daily life that we are prone to.

Considering this good of playing games I am thinking maybe that was part of the reason that before TV many people played games in the evening – a break from the fatigue and conflicts of their daily work.

In the book of Bob Sizemore *Nuggets of Wisdom*, where I am the responder, this effective Catholic counselor declares that family games are a wonderful thing.

# Day 49: Pacifism A and B

Ronda:

Insights:

St. Francis de Sales, a doctor of the Church, recommended games as a wholesome diversion for lay people. Why not be thankful for this fun part of my day instead of pridefully wishing I was above all that?

Reader:

Insights:

## DAY 48: The Perfect is the Enemy of the Good

This idea is attributed to famous thinkers but also to Robert E. Lee as a principle for battle-planning. At first sight it seems false. Isn't it good to try always for perfection in everything, from baking a cake to writing a book, to creating a dance, to framing a law? I have come to understand it in this way: when we aim for perfection we become easily discouraged and sometimes give up what we could do that would be good.

Here is an interesting example from my life as a writer. In public school in the 1950's we were taught to express ourselves in writing. This was a revolution. Before that emphasis was on correct grammar and spelling, not self-expression. Here is how the centuries old emphasis on perfect writing was the enemy of the good.

Brought up that way, most people who could have written good articles and books didn't even try since they knew they couldn't write perfectly. The Dominican Sister, Mary Neill, with whom I wrote 4 good books, told me that she couldn't write them without me. Why not write her own? She was paralyzed by fear of not writing perfectly. I still find what she wrote inspiring with the help of me, good, but not perfect.

Ronda:

Insights:

I am wondering what in my life now could benefit from realizing that the perfect is the enemy of the good? Exaggerated feelings of failure because of trying some 19 living situations after my husband died and none of them working? When I think, instead, of all the good that came to me in those places with those people, then I feel grateful instead of discouraged.

Wherever I go next, it will not be perfect, but surely it will be good.

And, oh my, isn't purgatory good even if it is not yet perfect heaven?

Readers:

Insights:

## DAY 49: Pacifism A and B

When I was teaching Ethics at Loyola Marymount University I wrote *Living in Love: About Christian Ethics.* Old copies of these can still be found, but the whole short book is now part of *The Way of Love*, published by En Route Books and Media.

Concerning the ethics of war and peace I was challenged by this dilemma. On the one hand we have the commandment Thou Shalt not Kill, and Jesus' insistence on turning the other cheek and loving one's enemies. On the other hand, God the Father, Himself, sent his people out to war against pagan enemies. And, when Christendom replaced the Roman Empire, battling enemies was not only accepted but praised.

So, why didn't Catholics become pacifists, defined as never killing any other person for any reason? The basic principle in Catholic ethics is that an evil person who is killing the innocent (for instance, a serial killer) or a country led by an aggressive leader (for instance, Hitler), forfeits the right to life.

I found it helpful to make a distinction between what I call Pacifism A and Pacifism B. Pacifism A holds that no one, especially not a Christian, can ever kill anyone ever. That has not been the teaching of the Church. If it was the teaching then no Catholic could ever become a soldier. Check out the Just War Theory in the Catechism of the Catholic Church.

Pacifism B is when a person states that he or she personally feels called never to kill anyone for any reason, but respects the right of others to do so for a just cause.

# Day 49: Pacifism A and B

Ronda:

Insights:

I think that for cholerics (those of angry temperaments, such as me) find it hard not to rush to defend justice using any means available. A humorous incident was watching the movie Rambo. When the hero lashes out at the enemy I leaped out of my seat yelling "Hurrah." It alarmed the Catholics who were at the movie with me.

Another incident was a woman who approached me after a talk and said she had been praying for me for 20 years because she was surprised how often the word "hate" came up in my previous talk!!!!

Even though I hold to Catholic teaching on reasons for defense against evil people or enemies of the country, I do think that I might pray more often and more deeply for peace in the world and in society.

Reader:

Insights:

## DAY 50: What is the Theme?

The last time I visited my dear friend, Alice Von Hildebrand, I asked her what specific advice she might give me.

"Go into encounters looking to see what is the theme!"

The opposite, too often my way, would be to plan what I want to say or hear about as is so characteristic of a teacher with a class. The theme could be sharing beautiful memories. It might be empathetically listening to someone else's dreadful problems. Playing a mutually beloved piece of music on a CD? I am linking this advice to what seemed many times to be the voice of Jesus telling me after something unexpected happened in a visit:

"We love to surprise you, Ronda!"

My co-author of *Always a New Beginning*, David Dowd, has been struggling with bi-polar, manic-depressive, disorder all his life. He says that not listening to see what the theme might be can result from mood-swings. If, out of depression, I am nurturing 'catastrophic thoughts' then I may want to lead a conversation immediately into manic jokes.

We ought to pray first to listen and what is called 'read the room' before launching into our own thing. This listening can lead to seeing what the unexpected theme might be.

# Day 50: What is the Theme?

Ronda:

Insights:

I determined that the theme of this particular day was to welcome lovingly one of my roommates coming back to our house from a trip. Starting right now I pray, dear Holy Spirit, let me listen empathetically when she speaks about her week away.

It worked! Alleluia!

Reader:

Insights:

## DAY 51: What is each of our Worst Defect?

"But who can detect all his errors? From hidden faults acquit me." (Psalm 19)

My book *The Way of Love* concludes with a 100-day marathon for becoming a more loving person. The last challenge is this:

Ask those who know you best from family, work, Church, first to tell you 3 things they love about you. Then ask them what is one defect they wish you would change.

Often, they will agree on the worst defect, and you will be surprised.

Examples:

The first time I tried this I was living with my daughter, Carla, and her family. I thought she would say my worst defect was anger. No. She said that I am a puddle-glum, that is, a total pessimist. So every time they plan something I pipe in with why it won't work!

I had never noticed that I did this!

I asked my husband. He replied, "Because you are a teacher, you are always grading everything we do – excellent, very good, so-so, poor, awful! I hate it."

Ronda:

Insight:

I asked a present-day close friend. She said: "Your worst defect is misinterpreting. I do some innocuous helpful little thing such as handing you a napkin and you bark out "you think I couldn't get that napkin myself?!!!"

# Day 54: God Alone is Enough

So, dear gentle Mary, I can't imagine you ever snapping at anyone that way. Help me, help me, help me.

Reader:

Insight:

## DAY 52: Why do you Think Irrational People will be Rational?

"With God all things are possible." (_____)

I asked a saintly man who was close to death what he thought I needed to change.

His answer was the title of this day's soundbyte!

He was referring to my relationship to a man who was not only a devout daily Mass Catholic, but also attractive because of his foreign accent, and sense of humor. However, he was a compulsive hoarder. His apartment was so cluttered, a visitor couldn't walk around except in a tiny path from kitchen to bed to bathroom. All the rest consisted in piles of books and boxes and old soda bottles, etc.

I would talk about this addiction with his friends and keep thinking I could convince the man to de-clutter just because it would be so much more attractive to visit him.

All those in 12 step programs are taught that addiction does not yield to practical advice by well-wishers. I like to joke, however, that someone else is looking at me and wondering why I stick with my irrational addictions such as being a *Talkaholic*! (See my recently published booklet *Talkaholics*) or picking my fingers (a habit since childhood).

"With God all things are possible." When we admit that we are out-of-control addicts and turn ourselves over to God He certainly can lessen our irrational ways and sometimes even eliminate them.

# Day 54: God Alone is Enough

Ronda:

Insights:

Dear Jesus help me to stop analyzing the behavior of irrational people I know and love. Instead show me gentle, peaceful ways to help them with small improvements.

Reader:

Insights:

## DAY 53: Loving even when you can't Like???

My dedicated widow friend, a counselor, Marti Armstrong, said:

"You can still love people even though you don't like them at certain moments when they annoy you."

Interesting and surely true. Certainly a parent doesn't stop loving his/her child because of annoyances! We love pets even though they sometimes bite or scratch. Most spouses find each other annoying. "I don't like you when you argue with me in front of the kids," for example.

It seems to me that the grace would be if I would be able to show my love when I am annoyed by not over-reacting but saying something gentle such as:

"Dear little daughter, we love you. Notice, though, that your father was taking a nap and when you yelled so loudly at your brother, it woke him up."

"Honey, you are a fine cook, but when you leave the stove for half an hour to talk to a friend on the phone in the middle of making dinner, the meat comes out a little tough."

Ronda:

Insight:

Guardian angel, do help me to overcome annoyance by showing love.

# Day 54: God Alone is Enough

Reader:

Insight:

## DAY 54: God Alone is Enough

These famous words were found in a bookmark of St. Teresa of Avila. They were made into a beautiful song of that title in Spanish: Nada te turbe. "May nothing disturb you, God alone is Enough." The song was composed by the Taize community. Search on the web for Taize you-tubes to listen.

I love the words and the song so I made them into the title of a booklet I wrote of the words that seemed to me to come from the Holy Spirit in the middle of the night during a period of a few months in the year 2008. When writing the sequel to my autobiography called *Further Along the Way* I included the whole sequence.

As I always explain in my journals, saying that The Holy Spirit told me something doesn't mean I am absolutely sure this was a revelation from the Spirit. I believe these messages are from God most of all because they are much better than anything I ever write or say!

May 14, 2008

Holy Spirit:

We (the Trinity) need the moral law because humans are so greedy about trying for heaven on earth in following their illusions that worldly goods will make them happy, such as stolen possessions or the pride of fame.

Just the same, it is not as if once someone sins we give up on them and totally reject them. No. We let them live in the consequences of their wrong choices. The 'righteous' want to see a clearer punishment, such as the immediate destruction of the body of this sinner. This is because the 'righteous' are tempted and jealous of the seeming good the sinner got by breaking the law…

Do you not see how Jesus tried to unmask these double evils by condemning greed and lust but also condemning self-righteousness?"

May 18, 2008

Holy Spirit:

Your homes, your doors, our arms, should be open wherever possible. How sad. So many locked houses and locked up personalities, as you say. Yes, sometimes locks are necessary. We know that, but it should be a sadness for you that this is so.

The house of Jesus, Mary, and Joseph was always open. The heart of Mary was wide open to the Incarnation in her constant prayer: she let God stretch her – now you are rightly calling her the spiritual mother of the world…the mother of a family always knows when one does not come to the dinner table. We miss you when you don't come to the Eucharistic table.

May 24, 2008

Holy Spirit:

When you are in a battle for the cause of truth, for Christendom: or to witness to your own personal values, you have an arsenal of words, your favorite weapons…words of Ours to bolster your truth with authority, sometimes taken out of context. I am the Spirit of Truth. When in conflict, I want you to come to Me with the openness of the poor in spirit…to let the truth shine through you, You have to be less defensive and really seek Me to give you the words that pierce, not like a dagger of hate, but like a two-edged sword of LIGHT.

Ronda:

Insight:

Rereading these messages from so many years ago I realize how much I still need to live out these truths.

About the words of the song Nada te Turbe – do not be disturbed – my twin-sister Carla, the sacred dancer, helped me with anger by giving me a hand movement for use whenever I was in a conflict with her or others:

Clasp the fingers of your hands into each other. Then twist them around a few times. Then let go and extend your hands outward and upward singing "Solo Dios Basta" – God alone is Enough.

# Day 54: God Alone is Enough

Reader:

Insight: (Does anything you read in the above fit with your own life right now?)

## DAY 55: Praying on Tippy-Toes or in the Heart

In the year 1969 I received the charismatic gifts of the Holy Spirit. (see my book *Why I am a Catholic Charismatic*)

Upon being prayed over by my twin-sister, I immediately received the gift of tongues. As well, it seemed as if a fire came into my heart.

I came into the Church in 1959 surrounded by Benedictine Oblates. They taught me to attend Daily Holy Mass and to pray the Liturgy of the Hours, short prayers from the psalms at different times in the morning, the evening and at night. I also tried to pray silently in my own words for 10 minutes each day.

Even though my mentors certainly prayed deeply and personally, I somehow said these prayers more from the mind and the will than from the heart. With those charismatic gifts came a sense of Jesus in my own heart waiting for me to come and speak to Him.

I liked to joke that before the charismatic gifts, I prayed by standing tippy-toes reaching into the sky. Afterwards I prayed by going into my heart.

I loved going to prayer meetings. Going to Holy Mass I tried to be at my best: silent, sitting still, then standing. But at prayer meetings we came in with all our problems showing in our faces looking for others to pray over us for healing.

I loved charismatic songs even though my favorite composer is Bach. For me Gregorian Chant appeals to my soul, post-Vatican II hymns to the psyche (as if I feel sad but "it's a brand new day"). Charismatic songs appeal to my gut as in – groaning in anxiety, throw myself into the arms of Jesus through song.

# Day 55: Praying on Tippy-Toes or in the Heart

Many decades later, wherever I move, I try to find a Charismatic prayer meeting for all those reasons.

Some of you readers may have had no experience of this, or a bad experience. Perhaps you could benefit from trying a prayer meeting for the first time or once more???

Ronda:

Insights:

Oh, thank you, thank you, thank you God for those charismatic gifts. Especially I pray for more of the gift of healing since I am such a wimp and wish always to relieve others of pain.

Reader:

Insights:

## DAY 56: The Divine Within?

During the 1960's a movement grew called New Age. Many former Church going Christians and Catholics, and Jewish believers, branched out to experiment with new ways of praying. Some of these were from Eastern religions such as Zen and Hinduism, especially yoga.

"The divine within," that is Scriptural, was often used to explain why most New Agers were not going to regular traditional services but praying instead in their own rooms or together with others to unite with the Divine Within.

I wrote a novelette called *The Messiah of the Metro Café* where the hero is a Jewish background 'guru' figure. Some seminarians studying for the priesthood near the café where the "Messiah" hangs out evenings, dialogue with him.

The Divine Within is a topic for such conversation. Here is an excerpt:

(Paul (a seminarian) asks the New Age guru):

"Michael, what is your favorite adjective for what God is like?"

Michael dark brown eyes shined with joy. "That's easy! God is all."

A seminarian, sarcastically retorted: "Oh, you mean God is a mosquito and God is even S.H.I.T?"

The expression "The God Within" can be made fun of in a like manner. As in, "You mean that God is inside each of your toe-nails?"

But, it can be better when dialoguing with New Agers to talk about the Divine Within as meaning that a creative spark of the personal God the Father is in everything in a mysterious way.

# Day 56: The Divine Within?

Ronda:

Insight:

    I am thinking now that if I was talking to a New Ager I would give personal witness to how I experience Christ, who is God, coming right into me in Holy Communion.

Reader:

Insight:

## DAY 57: Contraception - Why it is Wrong

One of the most controversial issues in the Church is contraception. Having sexual intercourse, and at the same time blocking the possibility of conception of a baby has always been taught to be wrong.

In my book *Living in Love: About Christian Ethics*, now part of *The Way of Love* I tried to find new ways of showing why that is wrong, including the pill that doesn't pose a barrier in the same way as condoms and diaphragm do. I also try to explain why even though in natural family planning the couple has sex but trying not to get pregnant is not the same.

Here are two images as I use:

Since being able to be a mother is a gift from God, a woman should view her fertile time as her glory time. She needs to tell a husband or any man that if he wants to enter into her body at that time he should be wanting to be a father.

It is winter. A boy receives a beautiful bicycle for Christmas. Upset that he can't ride it right away in the snow, he takes a hammer and wrecks the bike. Instead, he should postpone the ride until a good time and leave it in the basement. So, at a time when having a baby is deemed for serious reasons not a good idea, postponing conception by not having sex at the fertile time is good, but smashing up the destroying the sperm or egg's ability to reach each other in the sex act is not.

# Day 57: Contraception - Why it is Wrong

Ronda:

Insights:

    Nowadays quite a number of doctors do not recommend the contraceptive pills since they can have very bad side effects. Natural family planning has become the most successful way to postpone pregnancy. However, that is only if the couple is willing to abstain for about a week during each month. Some couples blame the method if they become pregnant when it is their own choice to take a chance.

Reader:

Insights:

## DAY 58: Absolutizing Trivia

I thought of this strange sounding phrase only recently. I put it in an article soon to be published by Homiletic and Pastoral Review about experiments in cooperative living for the elderly.

When planning to live with other people not of the same birth or adoptive family, we realize that we are going to have to adjust to new differences in character and personality. All newly married couples experience this. If they remain together they will have figured out, with the help of the grace of God, how to organize their daily life so that there is some kind of harmony of needs. In olden days before so many spouses were both working outside the home, a husband who needs more silence after a long day of work might take a walk before dinner. A wife might insist on going out to eat at least once a week.

Now, with singles living together for the first time, especially the elderly, conflicts may arise frequently over trivia. One person likes music turned up loud in the evening. Another person wants at the same time to read quietly in a nearby bedroom. One person likes everything very orderly, such as every different piece of cutlery in its own slot in a kitchen holder, where another likes to leave the clean ones all day in a pile on the dining room table.

Nothing strange about this. What is unexpected is the vehemence with which each person will justify that his/her way is better and has to prevail.

This is what I dubbed *absolutizing trivia.*

The most obvious solution to an on-looker will be compromise. Why not have a time, say 8 PM, when there is no music at all in the house? Before that no one should complain. Why not have a nice looking tray for cutlery on the table instead of in a drawer?

# Day 59: Who Won the Battle for the 20th Century Mind? 121

Sounds good, but you cannot imagine how much a person who has done something one way for 70 years will defend their way as absolutely better!

Ronda:

Insights:

From many years after my husband's death of living in diverse living situations, I have become an expert in detecting the absolutizing of trivia. I have not become an expert in compromise but I am a little better. For example, I was used to always throwing trash bags out of the apartment or house right after dinner since childhood. Now in a house where one member absolutely wants to wait until morning to include coffee grounds and bathroom garbage, I have become willing to wait.

I find that the old spiritual method of offering up trivial annoyance for the souls in purgatory is a big help.

Reader:

Insights:

## DAY 59: Who Won the Battle for the 20th Century Mind?

When I was asked to teach contemporary philosophy back in the last decades of the 20th century, I put together one of my best books. It was called *The Battle for the 20th Century Mind*.

Every chapter is about some disputed topic with excerpts from opposing thinkers such as:

- God doesn't exist or God does exist with analysis from the atheist Bertrand Russell and the believer Etienne Gilson.
- Determinism vs. Free Will: Skinner vs. Von Hildebrand
- Education - Progressive vs. Classical: John Dewey vs. C.S. Lewis
- Psychoanalysis of Freud and Jung vs. Viktor Frankl's Logotherapy
- Feminism vs. Christian Femininity – Simone de Beauvoir vs. Edith Stein
- Pacifism vs. Violence: Gandhi vs. Hitler and Stalin
- Pro-Abortion vs. Pro-Life: Margaret Sanger vs. Joan Andrews
- Etc. etc.

Who won? Truth is ultimately the victor and Christ is the Truth that Sets us Free. However, in terms of what the 21st century looks like it would certainly seem like a tie.

# Day 59: Who Won the Battle for the 20th Century Mind?

Ronda:

Insights:

I loved teaching that course because I could show my Catholic students how beautiful and strong truth was in opposition to so many ideas out in the culture at large. *The Battle for the 20th Century Mind* is available at En Route Books and Media.

Reader:

Insights:

## DAY 60: Hobbies and Identity

In the past whenever anyone was introduced to someone one would ask "What do you do?" The answer was to be your professional paid work or being a housewife.

And still, today, we tend to define ourselves by our work or our vocation: priest, sister, wife, mother, single…

However, I have been thinking that our hobbies are also part of our identity in interesting ways, especially when we are elderly so that our previous work no longer fills the largest part of our days.

My hobby has always been knitting. I was taught this as the girl and have been knitting all my life. I used to make little blankets for the grandbabies to be wrapped at their baptism with their names on it. Then I made Christmas stockings. Once I made a huge bedspread with sewed on, with sewed on outlines of the big moments of our married life. As I knit, I pray for the beneficiaries.

Today, a sweet moment was this: A 70 year old daily Mass man approached some of us old women: "My mother is now in her late '90's and can't knit any more. She has tons of old yarns. Does anyone want them?

Since I don't like to spend money for beautiful new yarns, but like to make crazy quilts of any yarn given to me, I jumped at the chance. Having put together old squares this old woman had made and then adding others knit by me with her yarn, I thought that she would be pleased to see the huge bedspread I made with her old yarns. Her son brought her to Mass today and I had the joy of showing her that her old wool had not gone to waste.

# Day 60: Hobbies and Identity

She smiled so sweetly seeing her old squares again and, of course, had suggestions from an old pro, how to make it better!

It occurred to me that my hobby had to do with my identity. How so? I am imperfect, like a crazy quilt, but kind of warm and colorful.

Perhaps a person with a hobby of playing baseball might have an identity that included responding to hard things like the baseball with a fast hit 'out of the ball park.'

A hobby of playing card games can fit with a person who is smart and who likes to guess what 'fortune' will bring.

Ronda:

Insights:

I am thanking God for the hobby of knitting. It keeps my restless fingers busy with something much better than picking them. Instead, I create things that people love to have as gift.

Reader:

Insights:

## DAY 61: Jewish Converts

Most of you readers know that I am convert to the Catholic Church from a Jewish but atheistic background. My story will come later in these Soundbytes when I tell you about my autobiography.

I edited two books of stories of Jews who became Catholics:

*The Ingrafting: Stories of Jews who became Catholics amd*
*Bread from Heaven: More Stories of Jews who became Catholics.*

I also wrote the life story of the famous Jewish Convert, Charles Rich, called *Hungry for Heaven*.

Looking back, I find that most Jews who become Catholics include in their stories dramatic miraculous happenings. I think this is because given the history of persecution of Jews by some Catholics, it is almost impossible to overcome prejudice against the Catholic faith by most Jews.

Many years after putting those books together I was part of the formation of the Hebrew Catholic Association in the US. This group is founded with the idea that when a Jew becomes a Catholic he or she need not think of themselves as no longer Jews but more like Hebrew Catholics. You might check out that web-site, if you are a reader with a Jewish background or know such a person who might feel drawn to the Jewish Messiah, Jesus, and His Jewish Mother Mary, and step-father St. Joseph with all Jewish apostles.

# Day 61: Jewish Converts

Ronda:

Insights:

I came from a totally atheistic background with a mother who was Jewish but brought up as an atheist and a father whose own father was a Masonic Jew, never practicing Judaism, and a Christian mother.

Just the same I am culturally Jewish, of the New York City type. What is that? Argumentative, blunt, loud and pushy on the bad side. On the good side, intellectual, warm, and creative. As a Jewish-Catholic, I want always to cultivate by means of grace the good side not the bad side.

Jewish Jesus, Mary, and Joseph help me!

Reader:

Insights:

## DAY 62: Jesus and I are 'Bigger' than myself and any only Human Person.

Most readers will surely have heard of co-dependency. This is a personality problem that comes when someone is overly dependent on the love of another.

Think of anyone you know, if not yourself, who is always craving proofs of love from an idealized other – constant affection, words of affirmation, attention…

Tending in this direction myself, I was feeling mournful because I wanted a certain person to prove love in such ways and it didn't seem forthcoming.

In the middle of the night, Jesus seemed to give me this truth:

"Ronda, you with Me is bigger than you with that friend."

This fits in with St. Teresa of Avila's refrain "God alone is enough."
Even if we are deeply in love with Jesus, we still need friends of all kinds. What we don't need is to make any friend into a kind of pseudo-savior!

Ronda:

Insight:

As part of my usual surrender prayer to God and His providence I am going to specifically beg Him to help me let go of any strangle-holds on non-divine persons.

Day 62: Jesus and I are 'Bigger' than myself and any only Human Person.

Reader:

Insight:

## DAY 63: "Stop Dogpaddling in the Waves of Life, let Me Float you to the Shore of Eternity"

Another beautiful word I seemed to receive from Jesus some years ago after turning 80 years old.

For awhile I thought it meant that I was to stop writing and speaking and become a 'full-time' contemplative.

Not really. It seemed more that what was needed was to get away from any kind of frantic workaholic type of activism. To still speak and write but not compulsively – slowly, and gently.

I find many elderly people love those words when I mention them in talks. They also have trouble getting away from valuing each day too much in terms of how much they got done instead of the quality of their relationships and of their prayer.

Ronda:

Insights:

Ah, yes – how much more lovely to be floated than to dog-paddle! Whenever I stop and let Jesus, figuratively, take my hand, the day goes by more pleasantly. Such peace is easily interrupted when there are set-backs and even crises. But instead of upset being the norm it become an interlude.

Day 63: "Stop Dogpaddling in the Waves of Life, let Me Float you to the Shore…"

Reader:

Insights:

## DAY 64: Doubts about the Catholic Faith?

About 10 years ago I worked on a course with Dr. Sebastian Mahfood for the online M.A. at Holy Apostles College and Seminary. The course was about atheism. Out of it came the book: *Why be an Atheist if?*

Many believers in God and the Christian faith struggle with doubt. I think this is normal given the crisis in the world and the Church today.

When doubts float through my mind I think of the chief intellectual reasons I originally came to believe:

God's Existence: Based on St. Thomas Aquinas' Third Way, I think, since nothing around us had to be, in an infinite amount of time there would be nothing at all unless, there was an absolute perfect being at the foundation.

Christ is Risen: As C.S. Lewis showed in Mere Christianity so many decades ago: Jesus claimed to be God (He said he was I AM, the Hebrew words for God). Either he was a liar, a madman, or really God. Since there is nothing in the New Testament that looks like he was a liar or a madman he is God.

As well, the disciples who knew what crucifixion was, and most of them had fled from it, would never have risked it by preaching Christianity if they hadn't seen the Resurrected Lord.

On the problem of how there could be a God of Love when there is so much pain in the world, again I rely on C.S. Lewis' arguments in *The Problem of Pain*. If God chose to create free will beings then they can reject Him and do evil that brings pain. Given the promise of heaven for those who do good following Jesus, it is worth any amount of pain on earth to receive an infinity of joy in heaven.

# Day 64: Doubts about the Catholic Faith? 133

Ronda:

Insights:

Nowadays I often add the image of weaning. In olden days, they weaned babies from the mother's breast by covering it with tar. Pain is like the tar that weans us from this world.

Reader:

Insights: What are some of your doubts, if you have them, and what bring you back to faith?

## Twelve of my Favorites of my Books ☺

Let me Tell you Why!

While writing *Soundbytes*, I was questioning myself. Maybe it is just vanity to think anyone wants to read excerpts from my books. The Holy Spirit seemed to say:

> "We like your books, we inspired you to write them!"

So, for the next twelve days I will tell you more about my favorites. The easiest way to find them, free, used, published or online is to put in search Books of Ronda Chervin: En Route Books and the specific title.

## DAY 65: *The Church of Love*

The first book I ever wrote came about in this way. My first full-time position, teaching at a Catholic University in Los Angeles, California, I noticed that the students didn't like the books I assigned, my own favorites by other philosophers. I asked them what books they did like. One replied:

"Dr. Ronda, we don't like to read, we like to surf!"

The Holy Spirit, I believe, gave me the idea of writing a book about the Church based on an analogy to romantic love. Surely these students liked to be in love! I called it *The Church of Love.*

I made 12 copies and sent them to Catholic publishers. No one wanted it until Liguori took it.

Here are a few of the ideas students and other readers liked best:

Suppose you are dating someone and getting serious. However, this person never wants to go out with you on Saturday nights. Since in the US Saturday is date night you would think that maybe your friend loves someone else more than you who he/she dates on Saturday nights.

Now, here's the analogy. Sunday is the day set aside for Christians to get off work and be able to go to Church. So, if someone who calls themselves a Christian wants instead to play golf, watch baseball games, or surf more on Sunday than go to Church, Jesus could think they don't really love being with Him that much!

Another favorite. Suppose your fiancé announced that he/she loved to listen to you talk but didn't want to be close to your body even when you got married someday?

Here's the analogy. Some say they like to meet Christ in the Bible, the Word, but don't believe that He meant it literally to want to come right into their bodies with His Body and Blood, the Eucharist.

Eventually, *Church of Love* went out of print. However, the *Magnificat* meditation magazine of daily readings excerpts from it regularly. Each time Catholics come up to me in Church or e-mail me to say how much they loved those insights.

(I am not putting in space here for Ronda's and Reader's insights since that doesn't fit for these days. Feel free to use the space beneath each entry for your own notes.)

# DAY 66: *Voyage to Insight*

I love, love, love this book. The idea was a write an introduction to philosophy that could be a textbook for my students but also an outreach to Seekers.

It would use the image of a voyage as a way to contrast skeptical and Godly philosophies with lots of quotations from these differing views and wonderful illustrations. There is space for reader insights.

The table of contents gives you the idea of how the reader is to put together one's own philosophy of life on the Voyage:

Fitting out the Ship: Ideas to be Jettisoned, Deepest Truths

The Captain: Body/Spirit, Programmed/Free, Individual/Communal, Eccentric/Loving, Finite/Infinite, Temporal/Eternal

Navigating: with Logic, with Experience, with Intuition, with Faith

Shipwreck: Disillusion, Wounds, Despair

The Sun, Stars and Lighthouses: God, Wisdom Figures

Isles of Enchantment: Beauty, Romantic Love, Mysticism

The Utopian Island: imagining a perfect form of communal life

Homecoming: Outlining one's own Philosophy of Life

To my great joy 50 years later I met a former student in a super-market who told me he saved Voyage to Insight with his entries and still re-read it!!!

# DAY 67: *Feminine, Free and Faithful*

The 1970's was the decade where what was called feminism became popular. The idea was to protest against all the ways men exploited, discriminated against, and abused women throughout the centuries.

At Loyola Marymount University were I taught, we were asked to devise courses in Women's Studies to analysis this movement and provide Christian insights into the God's created feminine. There were courses in Psychology of Woman, Sociology of Woman, and mine: Philosophy of Woman.

The key readings I used were Simone de Beauvoir's *The Second Sex* (a kind of Bible of feminists) and Edith Stein's *Woman* (a pre-feminist compilation of lectures the famous Jewish convert Catholic philosopher given in the 1930's in Germany).

My own studies of these and other books morphed into my book *Feminine, Free and Faithful*. The thesis was that women could be feminine, in the best sense, and free, in the best sense, if they were faithful to the Holy Spirit.

Example: Think how Mary, Mother of Jesus as known from Scripture and the apparitions, was so warm, nurturing sweet, and beautiful, but also as strong as any man, because she was absolutely faithful to the Holy Spirit.

I make much use of figuring out what the stereotype of feminine and masculine is – positive and negative. When we speak of someone as very feminine we could mean such traits as being kind, empathetic, giving…but we could mean the negative traits such as silly and weak, also part of the stereotype. With masculine one could mean strong, protective, wise, but one could mean brutal, domineering and arrogant!

# Day 67: *Feminine, Free and Faithful*

My book includes examples of wonderful women.

Here is the delightful story of how my book got published by the newly founded Ignatius Press: Fr. Joseph Fessio, S.J. the Jesuit who started this publishing house happened to have studied in Europe with Cardinal Ratzinger. Before he became Benedict XVI, Ratzinger was head of the office in Rome for the defense of the faith. Fr. Fessio was visiting him and Cardinal Ratzinger asked him if his new press had anything about this new challenge called feminism. Fr. Fessio remembered that my manuscript had been lying on his desk.

So, I joke that I owe that book to Pope Benedict!

## DAY 68: *Kiss from the Cross: A Saint for Every Type of Suffering*
(republished with the title: *Avoiding Bitterness with the Help of our Heroes, the Saints.*

This book has turned out to be the one most loved by my readers. When our beloved son, Charles, committed suicide, at the age of 20, it was a dagger in our hearts and the worst suffering ever for us.

I had written many books about the saints and so I thought I would try to see how they had managed to get through their terrible sufferings.

The book is divided into chapters about various types of sufferings such as Doubt, Despair, Exploitation, Physical Pain. For each type of sufferings I found a key saint to describe. It gives us great hope to see how they themselves accepted those bitter sufferings.

I often point those in physical pain to St .Lydwine of Schiedham, a little known saint of the time of the plagues in Europe whose excruciating physical sufferings were given her along with tremendous joy because of the way she was shown by God that they would be used for the redemption of souls.

## DAY 69: *En Route to Eternity: The Story of Ronda Chervin*

I have told my story many times in talks. The version on the Journey Home of EWTN is often re-run. I have come to understand this: I rarely remember the specific thoughts of speakers but always remember the most dramatic parts of their stories.

Isn't life itself more like a story than a tract?

In my autobiography you can read about my unusual childhood as a twin, an atheist, and then a Catholic convert. I wanted to marry a man like St. Francis, but instead eventually married a Jewish atheist divorced playboy. His first marriage in Tijuana was dispensed in Rome and right after our honeymoon I conceived our twins. Many years later my husband became a Catholic, too.

Well, you already have snippets of the rest in this book of Soundbytes. Praise God who has blessed me with so much joy and brought me through so much suffering.

## DAY 70: *Spiritual Friendship: The Darkness and the Light*

I never thought I could get this book published but finally it was taken by Daughters of St. Paul because the editor had problems with spiritual friendship and identified.

In the stages of spiritual friendship described, there are attraction, mutuality or rejection, dangers of sin and breaking it off or wonderful union of souls.

It is especially dear to me because I was saved from a toxic friendship and went on to better and better ones.

## DAY 71: *The Widow's Walk: How the Widow Saints bring comfort and direction* (later republished as a grieving book entitled *Walk with Me, Jesus*)

Written shortly after the passing of my husband, I was amazed that my research revealed so many, many, widow saints from all around the world.

I trace their marriages (contrary to what I thought, many were happily married) their grief, and the vocations they found in consecrated life or in other forms of ministry.

The last part details my rule as a Dedicated Widow, a prayer to Mary, Exalted Widow, and Stations of the Cross for Widows.

## DAY 72: *Taming the Lion Within: 5 Steps from Anger to Peace*

This book, often employed by me in parish ministry, combines psychology of anger management with Catholic spirituality.

Steps are: Admitting I am an Angry Person, Identifying my Type of Anger, Understanding my Anger, Taming the Lion day-by-day, and the Lion lies down with the Lamb.

My computer savvy daughters put together an online workbook so other leaders could use the book effectively. The workbook is available online at: https://enroutebooksandmedia.com/tamingthelionworkshop/

# DAY 73: *The Way of Love*

This large book is a compilation of smaller booklets. The first part is about the nature of love, largely based on C.S. Lewis' concepts in his The Four Loves. Second is Overcoming Obstacles to Love about typical unloving attitudes and habits. Third is Making Loving Decisions and is my small Catholic ethics book *Living in Love.*

The 4th last part used often separately in parish ministry is a 100-day Spiritual Marathon. I have referred to these challenges several times in Soundbytes.

Readers seem to like especially the very concrete examples they can easily understand and try to grow by means of practical applications.

# DAY 74: *Last Call: Twelve Men who Dared Answer*

For many years I have taught philosophy at seminaries. The last time was at Holy Apostles College and Seminary in Connecticut. This was founded for later vocation men.

Thrilled by the stories of such seminarians I decided to help them write them down. So inspiring were they that EWTN had me interview some of them for TV.

Imagine this one: a young man in Peru is of the family of the concubine, not the wife, of a farmer. His father wouldn't even greet him on the street! He goes off to High School in Lima and is such a good student that he becomes the only man in his village to go to college. But he feels the tug of a vocation to the priesthood.

He asks God to send him as a sign a man on a white horse to tell him if he should go to the seminary instead of college.

Right away, a priest from this US order of late vocation priests rides in from the next town on a white horse and tells him that God told him to come and find this very young man.

Now he is Fr. Peter Luna, priest, canon-lawyer and head of the order!

# DAY 75: *Why be an Atheist if?*

(co-author Sebastian Mahfood)

I know very little about science so I was excited that Dr. Mahfood wanted to co-teach a course with me on atheism for online philosophy M.A. students. He was knowledgeable about all the scientific arguments for the existence of God.

I particularly loved researching about converts from atheism including some from Asian backgrounds.

# DAY 76: *Escaping Anxiety on the Road to Spiritual Joy*

(co-author Al Hughes)

Some years ago, I met at the Society of Our Lady of the Most Holy Trinity college in Corpus Christi, Texas, a man who converted to the Catholic Church from atheism and then studied counseling and also spiritual direction. He was part of a group for writers I directed.

Coming back to Corpus Christi years later I asked him to be my spiritual director. He noticed that I was suffering from anxiety. I found his advice so helpful I thought we should write a book together detailing my problems and his penetrating suggestions.

We sometimes give workshops based on the book. Every anxious person who reads it finds it extremely insightful.

## DAY 77: *Always a New Beginning*

(co-author David Dowd)

While I was teaching at Holy Apostles in Connecticut, I had a group reading *The Way of Love* and sharing. One of the participants was David Dowd. He was a man of an unusual background. He came from a Catholic family with severe emotional problems. They were in the insurance business. David worked for years in insurance including in administration for the Legionaries of Christ. He was divorced with one son. He was a street preacher for years and also a pro-life activist. Dave had been drawn in middle-age to attend the Tridentine Latin Mass.

We became friends. He was working with a book on spirituality and often talked to me about it. I read the book and these conversations morphed into a dialogue book called *Always a New Beginning*.

Essentially this book shows how to relate to natural beauty, to friends, to Christ in prayer, in such a way that our psychological problems, some very deep seated, don't prevent us from having a new beginning.

Most poignant to me, because of my son who committed suicide, was that David, had tried to commit suicide out of his bi-polar syndrome many, many, times. He had been saved from this degree of depression by a combination of group therapy and the beauty of the Latin Mass.

Being a street preacher, Dave talks to everyone he meets and gives our book out in grocery stores, restaurants, and on his walks through parks!

# Good-bye

It was suggested to my son, at age 19, by a mentor, to try reading one of his mother's books. Afterwards, he smiled and said:

"Gee, Mom, if you did everything you say in this book you would be a saint!"

So now, at age 86, scanning all my books for Soundbytes, I am kind of trying to be a disciple of myself.

Since I am absolutely clearly not a saint, what's the missing link?

Marti Armstrong, another Dedicated Widow with whom I have lived the last year, said it could be lack of total surrender. She joked that the word "surrender" enchants her, but the thought of really totally surrendering scares her to death!

Am I the same?

Pray for me!

And, as the old gospel song has it:

"If I get to heaven before you do, I'll dig a little hole and pull you through."

# Books I Wrote

(Some of these were translated into Italian, a few into Spanish, *Kiss from the Cross* into Korean, and a short version of *Way of Love* into Vietnamese)

- *Church of Love*
- *The Art of Choosing*
- *Prayer and Your Everyday Life*
- *The Spirit and Your Everyday Life*
- *Love and Your Everyday Life*
- *The Way, the Truth and the Life*
- *Why I am a Catholic Charismatic*
- *Voyage to Insight*
- *Victory Over Death*
- *Living in Love: Christian Ethics*
- *Hungry for Heaven: The Story of Charles Rich: Lay Contemplative*
- *Treasury of Women Saints*
- *Catholic Customs and Traditions*
- *A Mother's Treasury of Prayer*
- *Prayers of the Women Mystics*
- *Quotable Saints*
- *The Kiss from the Cross: A Saint for Every Kind of Suffering* (new title *Avoiding Bitterness in Pain with the help of our heroes the Catholic Saints*
- *Prayer-Poems*

- *Woman to woman: Handing on our Experience of the Joyful, Sorrowful and Glorious Mysteries of the Rosary (Originally Ronda's Part of Bringing the Mother with You with Sr. Mary Neill)*
- *Help in Time of Need*
- *Feminine, Free and Faithful*
- *En Route to Eternity: the Story of Ronda Chervin*
- *Called by Name: Following a Personal Spirituality*
- *Freed to Love: Healing for Catholic Women*
- *A Widow's Walk – now entitled Walk with me, Jesus.*
- *Spiritual Friendship: The Darkness and the Light*
- *One Foot in Eternity Journals 1993-2013*
- *Becoming a Handmaid of the Lord (Journals)*
- *Seeking Christ in the Sufferings and Joys of Aging*
- *The Way of Love* (a spin-off version of this was written by Stephen Bujno, entitled *The Ways of Love: Transforming the Person*)
- *Taming the Lion Within: 5 Steps from Anger to Peace*
- *Weeping with Jesus: The Journey from Grief to Hope*
- *Healing of Rejection*
- *Why I am Still a Catholic*
- *Further Along the Road: Sequel to En Route to Eternity*
- *9 Toes in Eternity*
- *The Comic Catholic*
- *Talkaholics: Fate or Work-in-Process*
- *Last Journal 2022*

**Ronda: Fiction**

- *Ties that Bind*
- *The Last Fling*
- *The Crisis in the Church: A Dialogue between a Magisterial Catholic and a Progressive Catholic*
- *The Messiah of the Metro Cafe*

Ronda co-author

- *Terri Vorndran*
- *Woman to Woman*

With Sister Mary Neill:

- *The Woman's Tale*
- *Great Saints, Great Friends*
- *Bringing the Mother with you: about the mysteries of the Rosary*
- *How Shall we Find the Father (and Don Briel)*

With Msgr. Joseph Pollard

- *Tell me Why - Answering to Tough Questions about the Faith*

With Eileen Spotts:

- *Becoming a Woman of You're 15 Week Guided Journal*

With Msgr. Eugene Kevane:

- *Love of Wisdom*

With Ross Porter:

- *Healing Meditations on the Gospel of St. John*

With Eugene Grandy:

- *The Summer Knight's Tale*

With Richard and Ruth Ballard:

- *What the Saints Said about Heaven*

With Al Hughes

- *Simple Holiness*
- *Escaping Anxiety Along the Road to Spiritual Joy*
- *What Now? A Road Map for 80 Year Olds*

## With Kathleen Brouillette

- *Spirituality for All Times: Readings from the Catholic Classics*

## With Sebastian Mahfood

- *Catholic Realism: A Framework for the Refutation of Atheism and the Evangelization of Atheists*
- *Why be an Atheist If???*

## With David Dowd

- *Always a New Beginning*

## With Bob Sizemore

- *Nuggets of Wisdom*

*Storyworth*: With Carla De Sola Eaton and Diana Jump

## Ronda Editor

- *The Ingrafting: Stories of Jews who became Catholics*
- *Bread from Heaven: More Stories of Jews who became Catholics*
- *The Holy Dybbuk – Letters of Charles Rich*
- *Holding Hands with God*

- *Fabric of Our Lives: How to Write your Legacy for Family and Friends*
- *Letters for Eternity (Charles Rich)*
- *Last Call: Twelve Men who Dared Answer*
- *Toward a 21ˢᵗ Century World View*
- *Why I am Still a Catholic (booklets) and*
- *Short Takes: Why I am Still a Catholic*
- *Give me your Heart: Preparing for Eternal Life by Charles Rich*

Blog for many years on Goodbooksmedia.

Some titles are free for postage only from En Route Books and Media: visit https://www.rondachervin.com. Almost all can be found used, Kindle, or softcover by searching online Ronda Chervin and the title.

www.ingramcontent.com/pod-product-compliance
Lightning Source LLC
LaVergne TN
LVHW061345060426
835512LV00012B/2566